With What Remains

With What Remains

A widow's quest
for truth in Rwanda

Lesley Bilinda

Hodder & Stoughton
LONDON SYDNEY AUCKLAND

Copyright © 2006 by Lesley Bilinda

First published in Great Britain in 2006

The right of Lesley Bilinda to be identified as the Author
of the Work has been asserted by her in accordance
with the Copyright, Designs and Patents Act 1988.

1

British Library Cataloguing in Publication Data
A record for this book is available from the British Library

ISBN 0 340 90873 4

Typeset in TimesNewRoman by Avon DataSet Ltd,
Bidford-on-Avon, Warwickshire

Printed and bound in Great Britain by
Bookmarque Ltd, Croydon, Surrey

The paper and board used in this paperback are natural recyclable
products made from wood grown in sustainable forests.
The manufacturing processes conform to the environmental
regulations of the country of origin.

Hodder & Stoughton
A Division of Hodder Headline Ltd
338 Euston Road
London NW1 3BH
www.madaboutbooks.com

Contents

Acknowledgements

I'm sure this journey would never have happened – and hence this book would never have been written – were it not for the vision of Jay and Phil Knox of Purple Flame Media, and Ray Tostevin of GRACE Productions Ltd. I would not have had the guts, the perseverance or the openings to pursue the search for Charles' killers had it not been for them. Considering how little we knew each other before embarking on an intensive month of non-stop working, living and socialising together, I am amazed at how well we rubbed along together. Inevitably the high expectations, time pressure and considerable stress sometimes brought about tension in our relationships, but I am enormously indebted to them for their patience, wisdom, determination and sense of fun. The documentary produced as a result of this journey – *Hunting My Husband's Killers* – is an accurate, honest and sensitive portrayal of my turbulent and disturbing search.

Huge thanks to my sister Sue for supporting me unfailingly during our month in Rwanda, to her family for releasing her, and to the rest of my family for their backing and love.

I'm greatly indebted to a number of people in Rwanda who made our trip possible and supported us in so many ways: Nicholas and Elsie Hitimana, for their self-sacrificial and practical kindness despite their busyness, arranging accommodation, transporting, making contacts, giving advice and especially their friendship; Bosco, our translator, fixer and buddy for his irrepressible enthusiasm and energy combined with sensitivity in his practical help; Bishop Mutiganda, Bishop of Butare, for his generous hospitality and behind-the-scenes arranging during our difficult days in Butare; Archbishop Kolini, Archbishop of Rwanda, for supporting our quest and for his wise pastoral care.

Thanks to my manager Gill Forrest at Ware Assessment Centre, for her flexibility in accommodating the unexpected interruptions to my working schedule and her sensitivity in coping with my struggles in the weeks after my return.

I have really appreciated the professional support of Debbie Lovell in debriefing after my return, as well as her ongoing involvement.

And finally, although it may be a surprise to them, I'm grateful to the staff at the Animal Rescue Charity in Bishop's Stortford for entrusting me with Rosie, a very traumatised and timid retired greyhound whose companionship and gradual blossoming over this past year have been the best therapy for me ever!

Foreword
by Fergal Keane

Lesley Bilinda would never cast herself in the role of victim. She is much too self-effacing, far too concerned with the suffering of others to play the part of the suffering widow. Yet she has endured an exceptional trauma: the murder of her husband Charles in the Rwandan genocide of 1994 and then the long search for his killers, a journey described in this book with courage and compassion.

The genocide created hundreds of thousands of victims. There were more than eight hundred thousand who were killed and the hundreds of thousands more who were wounded, raped and traumatised by witnessing unspeakable violence.

And then there is the category to which Lesley belongs: the widows of the Rwandan catastrophe. Had she been with Charles when the killers came Lesley would undoubtedly have been murdered. Being married to a Tutsi would have been enough to warrant execution in the eyes of the Hutu extremists.

She escaped the massacres only because she was on holiday in Kenya with her sister. We should be grateful that she is with us in the land of the living. Not only for the self-evident reason of celebrating a life saved by chance, but also for the powerful and moving testimony which she gives us in this book.

When a friend asked me what the book was about I answered quickly.

'It's a love story', I said.

But it is not only the story of Lesley's love for her dead husband but also for Rwanda and ultimately humanity. A book that describes the horror of Rwanda's one hundred days of terror should not help to boost your faith in humanity. Yet that is what Lesley manages to achieve.

When confronted with horror her responses are entirely human. She expresses anger and anguish. But she does not allow herself, or the reader, to languish in despair. Nor does she ever – and there must have been times when it was tempting – lapse into what Holocaust survivor Primo Levi called 'the bestial vice of hatred'.

On one level this is a book about a Scottish nurse and her relationship with a small African country called Rwanda. But the Rwandan genocide wasn't just about Rwanda. It was about all of us, our human weakness and cruelty and also the small brave acts that glittered like pearls in the gloom. Lesley's book is a brave act. She has delved deep into herself to convey a haunting human experience and some profound spiritual truths. Reading it will bring you sadness and consolation but above all a sense of admiration for an extraordinary woman.

Fergal Keane 2005

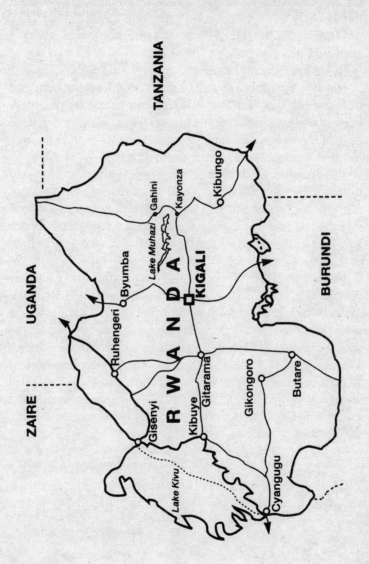

Introduction

This is a story about a journey. On one level it's a physical journey across Rwanda and back, searching for the truth of what happened to my late husband Charles; seeking to find those who killed him that I might in some way offer forgiveness. That was my purpose in going to Rwanda in March 2004. But in seeking to find the truth, I found instead a web of lies, deceit and betrayal. Through the close friendships I have with many Rwandans I realised that we shared the agony of never knowing what truth is or who can be trusted, the pain of reawakening past traumatic memories and the fear of intimidation and revenge.

Ironically, it was in that experience of betrayal that I did discover some truth – a revelation about Charles I had dreaded for years. Yet in that discovery I found that knowing the truth, however distressing it may be, could actually be freeing. So it is also a journey on a personal level, sometimes to the limits of my emotional endurance, wishing several times that I could give up and leave, but also inspired by faithful and honest Rwandan friends, who restored my belief in humanity and in God.

Some of the content of this book may come as a surprise to those who have read my first book. When I began writing *The Colour of Darkness* towards the end of 1994 I was extremely raw and traumatised. As well as the horrors of the genocide I was also struggling with problems in our marriage – issues so intensely personal I found them almost impossible to talk about, other than to a few very close friends. I was certainly not prepared to write them down for the whole world to read about. I reasoned with myself that people around me were finding it hard enough to cope with the news of the genocide, without adding our personal pain as well. I also felt – and still feel – a great sense of loyalty to Charles and to his family, and did not want to bring him or them into disrepute in any way whatsoever. But the major reason, as I later came to recognise, was that I was too ashamed to admit failure.

Over the past ten years my views have changed. The painful memories and the regrets remain, but I am learning to accept these as an inevitable part of imperfect life, and to live with them. The experience of returning to Rwanda and facing up to the many reminders of my failure was hard but healing.

Yes, my views have changed – and no doubt they will change again. For that reason I find it a very scary process to commit myself to paper, encapsulating my impressions, memories and perceptions into one very small space of time – a time which then stands still for ever after, even though my thoughts and my life move on. If I talk to someone who has just read *The Colour of Darkness*, several years after it was written, I sometimes get the impression that they think they know me. They don't. They only know the person I was when I wrote it, not who I am now. I have changed since then, and will continue to change. Yet by choosing this particular period of time to write again, I am restricted to my views as they stand at present. Perhaps my plea to the reader is to take what you find at face value, but recognise that I have the freedom to move on.

I also recognise that my understanding of situations and people I describe in these pages is limited to the here and now and could well change over time. For that reason I have tried to keep an open mind, aware that I have seen only a tiny snapshot into someone's life and circumstances. If I have misrepresented anyone, it was not intentional and I am indeed sorry. In some cases I have felt it prudent to change the names of certain characters in order to protect their identities.

A story is told of the world-renowned violinist, Itzhak Perlman, crippled by polio since childhood but famous for his outstanding ability as a player and for the tremendous joy he radiates through his playing. It is said that Perlman was giving a performance once when one of the strings on his violin broke. Undaunted, he somehow managed to continue to the end of piece. Later, when asked by a member of the audience how he had managed to keep going, he reportedly replied, 'Madam, my job is to make music with what remains.'

'Stuff happens,' as they say. Things go wrong in life, from the small disappointments and frustrations to the major life-changing catastrophes. The question to be asked when the crisis is over is not so much 'why?' – a question for which there is often no helpful response – but rather 'what next?' How will I respond to the situation facing me now?

I now feel I have much to be grateful for. Life's experiences have changed me, taught me to appreciate what I have and hopefully helped me to grow up a bit. But I never cease to be challenged by Rwandans I meet whose lives had been utterly devastated, who had almost lost the will to live, and yet who, with God's help, have picked up the broken pieces and turned them into something beautiful, free of bitterness or self-pity. You will meet some of them in the pages of this book. They are making music with what remains.

New Beginnings

The prisoner fixed his cold, hard, unflinching stare on me across the table. He was clearly a master in the art of intimidation. 'Madame,' he said, his eyes narrowing to a slit and the side of his mouth curling in a sneer, 'you have done me a great injustice. In a very short time I will be out of here, and then you will know that I am innocent.'

It was the end of a long day spent cooped up in a tiny crumbling office in Butare prison, south-west Rwanda, empty except for a large table and some rickety wooden chairs, a few sacks of potatoes and a pile of yellowing, insect-eaten papers. We had three prisoners on our list to interview, and this fourth was a tip-off from one of his fellow prisoners. I was completely exhausted. Concentrating for hours on end with my rusty Kinyarwandan and French, listening to graphically detailed confessions of how murders had been committed, searching for carefully worded questions which might just draw out an honest answer, and all the while trying to decipher where (if at all) the grains of truth were to be found. All this had used up every ounce of strength and courage within me.

The prisoner repeated his comment, slowly emphasising the words 'you will know.' A shiver ran down my spine. I was convinced he was lying, but suspecting someone of complicity in a murder is a very serious matter. This man might be in prison, and might stay there for a long time, but he would have contacts outside the prison, even outside the country. It would not be hard for him to track me down back in the UK. Talking to people around the country over the previous three weeks had left me in no doubt that violent and destructive intimidation of witnesses and survivors was indeed a possibility.

'I'm dreading this,' I had said to my sister Sue a few hours previously. 'I don't do confrontation. I can't think quickly enough on my feet, and I always lose in an argument anyway so what's the point?' But if I really wanted to track down my husband's murderer in a climate of lies and betrayal, where truth has lost all meaning, then I knew I had to face it.

I was back in Rwanda in April 2004, exactly ten years after the genocide during which my husband Charles had been murdered. My aim was to track down – and, if possible, forgive – whoever had been responsible for his death. But it was proving to be much more complex and disturbing than I had imagined.

For the previous nine years I had been trying to come to terms with the fact that I probably never would know the answers to my questions about what happened to Charles. He was 'just' one of up to one million people who had died in Rwanda in 1994 in the space of only one hundred days – ten thousand people *every single day* for three whole months. I wasn't even there when it happened, so how could I possibly expect to find out about the fate of one individual?

But things were changing in Rwanda. Over the past year or two a new court system had begun to be piloted. Based on the traditional Rwandan justice system these *Gacaca* courts involved the local population as witnesses and judges in the trials of local people suspected of crimes of genocide. New evidence was coming to light; some criminals were confessing their crimes of ten years previously. The truth was beginning to be known. Maybe, just maybe, I could at last find out exactly what had happened to Charles.

In the summer of 2003 I had had a phone call from the directors of two independent media companies – Purple Flame Media and Grace 4 Films. They had recently been filming in Rwanda and wanted to explore the possibility of making a documentary with me there. I was in the middle of a six-week retreat in splendid isolation in a cottage tucked away in the Scottish hills, but managed to drag myself away for a day to meet them. They flew up to Edinburgh and we spent the day sitting by the windows of two different cafes looking out at Edinburgh Castle and tossing around the possibilities.

Their idea was to take me back to Rwanda to try and track down Charles' killers and meet them face to face. As I thought it through over the next few weeks I had grave misgivings. For a start, even though the *Gacaca* courts in Rwanda were bringing new evidence to light and opening up secrets hitherto unknown, did I *really* think I could find out about Charles? He had been far from home when he was taken, in a town where few people knew him. The chances of there being anyone who saw what happened, *and* who knew him, were pretty slim.

The process of following his last days would be gruelling too. I'd have to visit the places he'd last been and talk to people about the little I knew of his last movements. This would involve hearing other people's stories and graphic details of events in 1994 recounted as if it were yesterday. That period of my life was absolute hell, and I had no desire to relive the memories and put myself through it again.

Then, if we did find his killers, how would I react? I had tried over the previous nine years to understand what forgiveness meant in this context and to put it into practice – as far as I was able. But how do you forgive someone you don't know? And it was one thing to contemplate the theory of forgiveness in a vacuum, thousands of miles away; it would be quite another thing to have to offer forgiveness face to face with a murderer – my husband's murderer.

And of course, even if we were to track them down and meet them, there was no knowing how they would react. The chances of them being remorseful for their actions and asking for my forgiveness were slim. Not unheard of – such had happened on a number of occasions in Rwanda – but I had to admit it wasn't very likely. More probably they would flatly deny any involvement with or knowledge of Charles. Or, worse still, suggest that it was deserved and they would do it again, given half a chance. How could I even contemplate facing someone like that? All in all, the idea of going back to Rwanda at this stage and for this purpose did not have much going for it. But on the other hand, how could I back away from the opportunity? Having tried for nine years to come to terms with never knowing the whole story, here now was a chance that I might be able to get to the bottom of it once and for all. Here was a possibility that I might be able to find some sort of resolution, let go of a little more of the pain of the past and move on. Perhaps it would be worth it for that. After all, surely it could never be worse than it had been in 1994, could it?

And what about going with a television crew? Certainly it would be tough to have a camera following me in my most vulnerable and painful moments, but there might be some advantages too. They might be able to use official connections and open doors that would otherwise be closed to me.

Over the next few months we continued to talk it through and gradually I came to the conclusion that, painful as it surely would be, it was something I had to do. My sister Sue was to come with me for support. She had been with me in Kenya when the news had come through in 1994 of the beginning of the genocide. Then, when I returned to the UK and moved in with her and her family, she had continued to support me and grieve with me through the months of horror that followed. It would make a huge difference for me to have her with me.

As the weeks drew nearer to our date of departure I found

myself focussing increasingly on Rwanda. My emotions were in turmoil. On the one hand I was dreading the journey ahead: what I might see, hear, discover; and whether it might send me spiralling downwards into the depths of despair again. But on the other hand I was excited about the prospect of being in Rwanda again, and especially of seeing my friends and family again – people whose lives I had shared so closely and who had remained dear to me for so many years.

Those years in Rwanda held such mixed memories for me: happy, carefree, innocent years; strong friendships built with families in the local community; the excitement of romance and marriage. But then the pain and loneliness of rejection and betrayal; the fear, hopelessness and despair. When I thought back to my life in the early months in Rwanda in 1989 and compared it to my life now it seemed like two different worlds. I had changed so much during and since that time. Would I still feel I belonged there? Did I ever belong there? Could so much change in fifteen years? In those early days I was enthusiastic, optimistic about life – and naive.

Stepping out of the plane at Kigali International Airport, a wall of heat hit me and I paused before negotiating the unsteady steps down onto the tarmac. I took a deep breath of the warm, heavy, smoky air. 'Mmmmm. The smell of Africa,' I thought to myself with great excitement. 'I'm back!'

1989 was my second time in Rwanda. The first had been a short trip as a volunteer a couple of years before – a taster to see if I could cope with the heat and the spiders (my pet hate) before signing up for a longer stint. How could I not come back? There is something about Africa – perhaps Rwanda especially – which gets under the skin of us Westerners, drawing us back and changing us forever.

It's not that I'd always had a hankering for Africa. It was more of a logical decision to go really. From a sheltered small-town Scottish childhood, studies at university had opened my eyes to the inequalities and injustices around the world. I remember being part of a student delegation lobbying my MP in the wake of the Willi Brandt report *North/ South: A Programme for Survival*, terrified in case I'd have to speak and wouldn't fully understand the issues, but believing passionately nonetheless that something had to be done about our unfair world.

So off I went to London to train as a nurse and then a midwife. Perhaps in this way I could offer something practical to play my tiny part in changing the world! Having previously studied French at university, I guessed it would make sense to look for a job in a French-speaking country. And if I'm honest, I also had a sneaking sense of adventure, a longing to branch out into something different and challenging. It was important for me to be in what I considered then to be 'God's will' for my life, and though I was not one for proof texts confirming God's 'call' to me, nonetheless I felt that this combination of factors made sense to me and before God.

And so it was that I found myself back in Rwanda in 1989, bumping along the pothole-strewn road that led to the village of Gahini, on the eastern edge of the country. To my shame I had found out virtually nothing of the history of Rwanda – only that there had been ethnic uprisings in the past, but for many years since then it had been a peaceful place. It was also an incredibly beautiful place. The journey between Kigali and Gahini took a couple of hours, leading us between gently rolling hills covered from top to valley floor with tiny fields of luscious green crops. On the hillsides small traditional mud houses with dried grass roofs nestled in among great stretches of densely packed banana palms, their huge, deep-green leaves rustling and tearing in the wind. Nearer the roadside some of the houses had brightly painted concrete walls and corrugated tin roofs.

And the people! People everywhere. Bunches of kids

running and giggling along the road, girls in royal blue dresses, boys in khaki shorts and shirts – school uniform, I learned. Brightly clad women striding out to market, laden down with babes strapped to backs and baskets piled high with bananas or sweet potatoes balanced steadily on their heads. Young boys, bare-footed, dressed in earthy-brown shorts and faded T-shirt or threadbare jumper, standing around with stick in hand, keeping half an eye on a handful of pregnant-looking goats. Men on rickety bicycles, the handlebars completely obscured by a great mass of lumps of feathers swinging around – barely-alive chickens on their way to market. And then there were the cows. Bony, scraggy-looking beasts with the most enormous horns sticking out at the sides, surely at least eight feet from tip to tip. Watching the speed at which they swung these mighty weapons around to ward off flies on their backs, I admired the bravery of the young boys looking after them – and made a mental note never to venture too close.

There was so much to take in, I felt as though I would burst with the richness of impressions all around – and with my excitement. This was to be my home for at least the next four years. It was almost too good to be true. In my innocence I had no thought then of what was to come during those years, experiences that would break me, and all but totally destroy my trust in humanity and in God.

I woke up on my first morning in Gahini to the sound of whispering voices and giggling very close by. Hang on, where was I? What was happening? I turned over in bed to face the bright morning sun pouring in through the little square window, barely restrained by the thin cloth hanging over it as a curtain. Ah yes, I was in my new home. Or rather, I was in John and Gemima's home.

My role in Gahini was to be co-ordinator of the Gahini Community Health Project – a job which would take me far out into the countryside, getting alongside the local population, learning about their problems and working with them to improve their standards of health. In order to do that effectively not only would I have to speak the local language – Kinyarwandan – fluently, but I'd also have to learn quickly about their way of life, challenges and frustrations.

The best way to prepare for this, I thought to myself while still in the UK, would be to spend some time living with a Rwandan family, learning from the inside, so to speak. John and Gemima had reluctantly agreed to host me. 'When we were asked about it,' Gemima told me some time later, 'we prayed about it, and felt God was saying it was what we had to do.' Perhaps it was just as well I didn't know about their hesitation at the time. I probably wouldn't have come! But it was understandable. Although there had been expatriates living in Gahini for most of the twentieth century, it seemed that they had not always been closely integrated with the local Rwandan population. This was the first time a *muzungu*, a Westerner, had asked to live with a Rwandan family, and John and Gemima knew there would be suspicions as to their motives. Were they getting lots of money? Would they be in favour with the other *bazungu* (Westerners) and be given better positions? How would they cope with the strange habits of a *muzungu* girl in their house? But being the gracious, godly and generous-hearted people that they are, John and Gemima took the plunge and I became part of their family. 'We have six children,' I heard Gemima tell a church gathering once, as she gave her testimony. I was confused. Having taken some days to work out which were their own five children, given that there were always so many children playing around their house, I didn't understand how they could now suddenly have six? 'Five of our own, and our sixth one is Lesley,' she explained to the crowd.

Both my 'parents' worked at Gahini Hospital – John in charge of the diagnostic laboratory and Gemima running the sterilisation unit. They were both also closely involved in Gahini church and in the local Scripture Union group, frequently heading off at weekends with a team to some distant parish to preach. Sometimes I went with them – but try as I might, I couldn't always share their enthusiasm or the encouragement they gained from such trips. For me it was more of an endurance test. Crouching for hours on end on a low wooden bench while preacher after preacher waxed lyrical, understanding no more than one in every hundred words –for me this was not the most memorable way to spend a Sunday. Nor was I very good at waiting till five in the afternoon for my lunch. But I did develop a great appreciation for big plates of boiled cassava, rice and beans, and mugs of piping hot, weak, sweet tea.

From John and Gemima's house it was a twenty-minute walk to the hospital. The working day began at 7 a.m., so that meant a very early rise in the morning. Well, six o'clock was pretty early for me to get up, but for the rest of the family it meant a much earlier rise. There was water to be collected from a nearby lake (no taps and running water in the house or even nearby); the fire had to be started in the outside kitchen for cooking the sorghum porridge and the tea; the cows had to be taken out to grass – and all this *before* going to work or school.

I must admit I was not at my most helpful or enthusiastic first thing in the morning. But although I was included as part of the family John and Gemima never put any expectations on me to do any of the daily jobs, insisting instead on treating me more as the honoured guest much of the time. As well as the morning porridge we often had fresh bread for breakfast – a luxury, I later discovered. And, what's more, to spread on the bread they had bought not only a tin of Blue Band margarine (with a strangely bluish tinge to its electric yellow contents) but *also* a jar of jam. Although it probably meant they had to do without something else, they knew that this was what we *bazungu* were used to, and wanted to help me feel as much at home as possible.

Communication in these early weeks was pretty basic. Although John spoke pretty good English, and Gemima a fair bit of French, they had been encouraged not to use it with me, so that I'd be totally immersed in the local language. Hearing only Kinyarwandan spoken by Rwandans around me all day was undoubtedly the best thing for my language learning in the long run, but in the short term it was very hard going. As all my friends and family know well, I do like to talk and express myself. So conversation that was limited to 'Good morning, did you sleep well?' 'What is this?' and 'I like beans,' left me with bursting with frustration at not being able to put words to my impressions, thoughts and feelings.

Many a time, as we met with John and Gemima's friends along the road or sat chatting in the sitting room, someone would make the comment about me: 'She's very quiet, isn't she.' 'NO, I'M NOT,' I wanted to shout out (if only I could!). 'You don't know me! It's just that I can't understand you and I can't talk to you, so what else can I do at this stage but sit quietly in a corner and smile sweetly!' But the lifesaver for me was that my colleagues at the hospital spoke French, and there was also a handful of Brits living in Gahini, so I did have opportunities to express myself to my heart's content elsewhere.

Over the early months I guess my need to communicate, to hear and be heard, probably played a big part in developing my sense of belonging in the local community, and in John and Gemima's family in particular. The only way I could really get to know people and understand the issues facing them would be if I could speak their heart language. And the best way to learn to speak their language would be to spend time with them. Time is a commodity that never seems to be in short supply in rural Rwanda. Few people have watches or clocks and many don't travel beyond the village other than to visit relatives or attend a wedding or funeral – and often on foot. Taking time to visit, to chat, to find out the news, seemed to take priority over pretty much everything else. It was hard for me as a task-oriented Westerner coming from a culture where 'time is money' to adjust to a people-oriented culture. One day, having tried for the umpteenth time to explain to an elderly gentleman why I was too busy to come and visit him and his family at their home this week, he shook his head wistfully. 'Ah, you people don't love us as the old missionaries did,' he sighed. 'They used to visit us all the time.' I felt somewhat reprimanded!

But visiting was a significant part of my work, and I really enjoyed that. In the Gahini Community Health Programme I worked very closely with Anatolie, a trained social worker and mother of two gorgeous little girls, Mireille and Liliose. Our aim was to improve the quality of life and reduce ill health in our catchment area. There were a number of different elements involved, but the core of the project was the training and supervision of a team of around fifty voluntary community health workers – or *Agents Sanitaires de Base* (ASB). Each ASB was elected by their own community and worked in their home area. They were expected to visit the families in their area regularly, talking with them about their health problems and trying to help them find ways of improving their health. Most of the visiting was done by the ASBs themselves, but Anatolie and I tried to make time to visit each of our areas and spend time with the workers, focussing particularly on families where the ASB had encountered difficult issues.

Some of the areas we went to were quite remote so we had to take the car part of the way. We had a spanking new Toyota double-cabin pick-up truck, but unfortunately not the four-wheel-drive variety. Home visiting journeys tended to be a bit, well, interesting… Many a time the ASB with us would assure me that the narrow, winding path ahead was fine for vehicles and regularly used – only for me to find, as I inched forward over the ruts and bumps, scratching the paint off on both sides with the prickly bushes, that there was an enormous ant-hill in the middle of the road or that the recent rains had washed the road almost completely away.

Why hadn't I done that 'Driving-in-the-sticks-for-beginners' course before I left the UK?

Very few vehicles would be seen in these remote areas – usually only trucks collecting produce for sale in the markets. The terrain was really much better suited to walking, which was fine by me! The scenery around was fantastic and I loved walking along the winding paths over the hills with Anatolie, sun in my face, chatting to the women working in the fields and to the children playing outside their homes.

No doubt it was a daunting sight to the families chosen for a visit to see a delegation of three heading purposefully in their direction – especially as one of them was a *muzungu*! But Anatolie had a great knack of putting people at their ease. We would sit together on a rickety wooden bench or a rush mat spread out for us on the earthy ground while Anatolie laughed and chatted with the mum on issues as diverse as family planning, the value of growing vegetables, updating the children's vaccinations or preventing diarrhoea. Even when my Kinyarwandan was eventually good enough to hold such conversations myself, it was still much better to leave this to Anatolie. She was brought up in the countryside and understood the issues and difficulties facing these hard-working women. They respected her and listened to her – and occasionally even put into practice what she suggested!

After a few years, Tearfund (the Christian relief and development organisation with whom I was working in Rwanda) gave us a grant to buy a motorbike for the project. It made sense economically for journeys like these home visits, and was much more practical for negotiating the narrow paths. By this stage I was married and my husband Charles also had a motorbike for his work. I loved travelling with him on the back of his bike and was keen to learn to ride it for myself. So we struck a deal. He would teach me to ride a motorbike and I would teach him to drive the Toyota.

Living out in the countryside gave us plenty of space to practise. Our favourite place was the old road that led from

Tanzania to Uganda, winding along the shore of Lake Muhazi. The smart new tarmac road had been built by the Chinese only a few years before, so the old one was still in reasonable condition. It wasn't used much though, and the main hazards seemed to be small groups of cattle coming down to the lake to drink. We kept a respectful distance from them and their horns! But I expect the boys tending them kept their neighbours well amused with the gossip about a *muzungu* girl driving a motorbike with a Rwandan man as passenger.

Riding a motorbike out in the sticks with Anatolie on the back caused a bit of a stir too. It was very unusual to see women riding motorbikes and not surprisingly so. Women in the countryside don't tend to wear trousers, so trying to find a way to get on the machine and stay on when clad in a long wrap-around cloth, and still remain respectable, was quite a challenge for Anatolie!

Once when I went to visit Charles, not long after we had first met, I was surprised to see his motorbike parked in his sitting room. This, apparently, was where it lived at night-time. Actually, although it looked a bit odd, it made a lot of sense. No sitting room in Gahini had wall-to-wall carpeting. In fact, no sitting room had carpets at all. It would have been totally impractical given the mud and dust brought constantly into the house. The floors were cement, easy to sweep and wash, so any mud brought in by the bike could easily be washed away in the morning. And the alternative – leaving it outside overnight – would probably mean that it would have disappeared by the morning.

Charles took his responsibilities seriously. He was a hard-working, conscientious English teacher in the local church secondary school, but he had lots of friends outside of work too. It seemed to me that any time I popped in to see him (his house was conveniently only ten minutes' walk from mine and en route to Lake Muhazi where I sometimes went to swim), he had a room full of visitors chatting and laughing and sipping mugs of tea. And he could never say 'no' to a request for a lift on his motorbike – whether it was to bring a friend's sick relative to hospital or give a colleague a lift home on a dark night. This warm-hearted, generous spirit was a side of Charles I really loved as I got to know him better. But after our marriage it also turned out to be a source of growing tension and my naivety turned to suspicion as I struggled with his frequent long absences from home.

In fact, it wasn't just the latter months of our marriage that were characterised by conflicting emotions and mixed memories. My whole time in Rwanda, as I reflect on it years later, was a jumble of mixed experiences and feelings that have lodged very deep within me. It was a place where I felt I belonged and where I was loved and accepted, where I married and settled. But it was also a place where I discovered rejection and betrayal, and the most painful loneliness of my whole life. And in the midst of the worst time, just when I thought I could take no more, the genocide began. One hundred days of slaughter swept the country I had come to see as my home. Charles was murdered. Anatolie and her husband were murdered. John and Gemima and their family fled the country – as did nearly two and a half million people – and lived in squalor as refugees. I became a 'refugee' in my own country, Scotland, desperate but unable to get back to Rwanda.

And now, ten years later, I was back in Rwanda, trying to find the missing pieces of the jigsaw. Would I at last be able to find the truth of what happened to Charles? Would I find Anatolie's orphaned daughter, Liliose? Would I still feel I belonged in Gahini again and with John and Gemima's family?

The next three weeks would provide some answers to these questions, but often not in the ways I had imagined. And there were also some unexpected and disturbing discoveries waiting for me just around the corner.

2

Making Plans

'*Good grief – what a day!*' I wrote in my journal on Friday 26 April, two days before our flight to Rwanda. '*Live interview with BBC Radio 4 Today programme at 8.40 this morning and the phone hasn't stopped ringing since.*' It was my last day in the office, but I wasn't getting much work done that day. Several newspaper and radio interviews later, with promises of more to come on our return, and I was feeling quite exhausted and bamboozled. 'If this is what it's like just thinking and talking about the visit,' I commented to a bemused colleague, 'then how's it going to be when I'm actually there?'

I was finding it strange that there should be such interest in this trip. When, several months previously, Tearfund's media department had offered to act as my agent and co-ordinate the media interest around the time of the tenth anniversary of the genocide, I had kind of laughingly said 'yes', expecting that they wouldn't exactly be overworked on my behalf! But that was before I knew of my return visit and the documentary in the making.

It was hard to marry up what to me was an intensely private and personal quest – that of trying to retrace my late husband's last days and meet those responsible for his death – with the very public nature of the media interest. True, I was about to spend the next four weeks being followed everywhere by a camera, so I had been obliged to think it through, at least to some extent. But somehow that seemed a bit different. Over the past few months of meeting and working together with the crew – Ray, Phil and Jay – we had already built up good relationships, and they felt more like friends to me now. So it was often easy to forget that my personal fears, hopes and questions might one day be laid bare to the whole world (well, maybe the tiny part of the world that might be vaguely interested!).

Perhaps the journalists' questions were obliging me to focus on the harrowing challenges ahead of me, whereas I had been tending to think more about the positive aspects of being back in Rwanda. I was excited at the prospect of seeing John and Gemima and all their family again. I was looking forward to eating goat kebabs, sorghum porridge (yes, honestly!) and endless supplies of mini bananas. It would be fun to browse around the marketplace again with all its life and colour and vibrancy, and to bargain with the stall-holders in Kinyarwandan. It was certainly easier to reflect on these fun things than on the prospect of visiting a genocide memorial site, interviewing mass-murderers or uncovering shocking details of atrocities. But of course the journalists were more interested in the latter than the former so I was forced to face the reality of what I was likely to encounter in the next few weeks. And that was hard.

But the next thirty-six hours of last-minute preparations and packing allowed me little time to think about what lay ahead, good or bad.

It was good to be travelling with others. I had been more used to long-haul flights on my own so it was quite a luxury to be able to walk around the airports unencumbered, taking it in turns to guard the piles of hand-luggage. Long-haul travel is such a weird experience: drifting in and out of sleep on and off the ground; losing myself for a couple of hours during the in-flight movie; groggily fixated by the tiny plane on the world map screen on the seat back in front of me, as it inches its way over countries and continents, wondering what life would be like immediately below us; wandering aimlessly around the airport shopping malls among other bleary-eyed travellers.

It was still the middle of the night when we arrived in Nairobi and we had seven hours to wait there. The first priority was to head straight for a café area which Jay and the gang had discovered on a previous stopover here. Not that any of us were interested in the food, but this café had proper chairs. Not hard-backed, upright hard plastic ones but flat, padded plastic ones that fitted exactly together in a row. You could stretch out horizontally on these chairs without ridges of hard plastic digging into your ribs whichever way you turned. And what I wanted more than anything else at this precise moment was to stretch out horizontally. But I also wanted to check out what was new in the airport tourist shops, so after a couple of hours of horizontal therapy, drifting in and out of reality, Sue and I wandered off to explore the surroundings. Coming to Kenya from Rwanda used to be a real treat. There was so much more available in the shops here than there had been in Rwanda. It was fun to be a tourist again, searching through the brightly coloured T-shirts splashed with safari animals or *Hakuna Matata*, feeling the smooth, polished elegance of a tall, carved giraffe or impala, my eyes flitting hungrily from batiks to jewellery, from *kikoyo* wraps to tiny flip-flop keyrings. Even in my semi-drowsy state I was excited to be back in Africa again, and I wanted to take it in all at once.

The crafts and knick-knacks on sale here seemed much the same as they had been a few years before on my last visit. But would there now be similar things available in Rwanda, I wondered? There had been so much progress and change in Rwanda over recent years and maybe that would be reflected in new lines and designs in the tourist craft market. What else might have changed? Would I still recognise the place? It was almost five years since I'd been back but somehow it felt like much longer than that.

Finally, after another stop in Burundi, we were nearing the end of the journey. It had seemed to take a very long time getting to that point. I looked down on the familiar landscape: rolling green hills as far as the eye could see; tiny houses dotted all over the hills with clumps of trees and banana palms; the brown, twisting snake of a river... Urrgh! The Akagera River. Suddenly images of ten years ago came to mind at the sight of the river – bobbing heads, bloated bodies, rags of clothing all being swept along in the frothy muddy waters. The Akagera River in those days had become a mass grave for thousands of victims shot, clubbed or macheted to death during the horrors of the genocide.

Flying low over Kigali airport runway I scanned the tiny figures on the balcony, wondering if anyone had come to meet us. My mind flitted briefly back to the same balcony in the early 1990s, out of bounds to the public but packed instead with sandbags and soldiers. So many images, memories and feelings all jumbled up together. It would be easier to block them out altogether than face up to the confusion within me. I knew I would have to face them soon, but not just yet.

There were only about thirty people disembarking in Rwanda so the customs officials could take their time and search everyone's luggage. We had nothing illegal, but Sue and I did have lots of gifts for the folk we would be visiting – towels and clothes, children's toys, crayons and colouring books, assorted toiletries and calendars, and of course lots of chocolate. And they were all carefully and tightly jammed into our suitcases, so if the customs official did much rummaging around we'd never get the cases shut again. I began chatting to him in Kinyarwandan as we heaved the cases onto the table. He barely looked up from his work, indicating to me to open the first suitcase. Perhaps it was no longer a novelty to hear a *muzungu* speak Kinyarwandan. I continued chatting, mentioning that we were carrying gifts for my friends in Gahini, where I used to work.

That did the trick! Just one mention of Gahini, and a smile broke out on his face. Although a tiny place, Gahini had been known throughout the country for decades for the high standard of medical care practised there and the compassion of the hospital staff. It also boasted a rehabilitation centre for people with disabilities – the first of its kind in the country – where people from all walks of life and from all over Rwanda had seen their lives transformed from helplessness to independence. Maybe this customs official had had a member of his own family treated there? Who knows? But at least he seemed to believe that anyone associated with Gahini must be OK, so he shut down the lid of my case again and waved us through. First hurdle over!

To my enormous relief, as we emerged into the main hall, there were the familiar, welcoming faces of Elsie and Nicholas and their delightful little children. Lots of hugs all around, the inevitable 'yes-we're-tired-but-it's-great-to-see-you-again' exchanges, and trying to remember when we'd last seen the children and how old they must be now. I had known Elsie and Nicholas for many years. Elsie had been bridesmaid at our wedding and then during the genocide they had both had to flee the country and had ended up eventually in Scotland, where Nicholas studied at Edinburgh University. They were the first people to be supported through their studies by the charitable trust we set up in memory of Charles – the Charles Bilinda Memorial Trust. Now they were back working in Rwanda and over the past few months had been extremely helpful in making contacts and arranging our trip.

Also there to meet us was Bosco, a young lad with an open, warm face. He'd been the translator and fixer for the crew when they came out on a research trip earlier in the year, and would be working with us again over this month. He was clearly delighted to see Ray, Jay and Phil again.

Fortunately, given the vast amounts of equipment and

luggage we were travelling with, there were two vehicles to take us into town – the four-wheel-drive Pajero bought by Nicholas and Elsie's many friends in Scotland for his work with widows and orphans, and another hired by Bosco. I sat in the front with Nicholas, hungrily devouring the familiar sights as he drove us into town. Lots of new buildings had sprung up over the past few years. There were sumptuous villas, fit for a James Bond movie, sprinkled over the hillsides just a stone's throw away from the old clusters of densely packed mud houses, which were separated only by steep narrow paths and had open drains running between them. High-rise, all-glass blocks had taken the place of two-storey, run-down brick buildings in the city centre.

But some things hadn't changed. The old parliament building, home to the small contingent of Rwandan Patriotic Front soldiers just prior to the genocide, was no longer in use but still displayed its peppering of bomb and grenade holes for all to see as they drove or walked past.

We drew up at the front gates of the guest-house of the *Église Presbyterienne au Rwanda* where we were to be staying for the first few nights. Looking through the open gates I was struck by a blast of colour from the wide beds of exotic flowers. Behind them, in a long low building, four or five bright blue doors divided the clean, whitewashed walls. It was a fresh, welcoming sight after a long, sticky journey. Our rooms were neat and clean, mosquito nets hung over the beds, a TV sat on a desk in a corner (and it worked), and in the large en-suite bathroom there was a bath and shower, with functioning flush toilet and, luxury of luxuries, hot running water! Some things had certainly changed for the better in the past ten years.

That evening, after a meal at Nicholas and Elsie's house, I scribbled some notes in my journal. Even in just these first few hours in the country my swings of emotion had been huge – not in outward expression, but in the inner feeling deep in the pit of my stomach, which changed from one minute to the next, with only the tiniest cue. '*Driving from the airport,*' I wrote, '*everything seemed so familiar and normal. I felt how good it would be to live here again.*'

Yet, only a few hours later, driving round to Nicholas and Elsie's in the dark, I was gripped by anxiety. Maybe it was the sight of the bars on their windows, or the high wall around their house and big metal security gates, opened to allow the car in then clanked shut again immediately after us. I couldn't help but think back to those who'd tried to hide in 1994. Even the highest walls, strongest locks or most ferocious dogs provided no security whatsoever for those being hunted down. So often back then I'd imagined the terror of trying to hide and now, back in the country, these images were never far from my mind.

And then there were the conversations in Nicholas and Elsie's house. At times when they were talking among themselves in the family I lost the gist of the conversation entirely. My Kinyarwandan was rusty and didn't cope well with several folk in a group all talking at once. I felt lost and left out – and it reminded me acutely of the many times Charles and I would have had a sitting room full of visitors all talking at once and losing me completely. How desperately I had wanted to belong, yet felt an outsider even in my own home. Strange how little incidents of many years previously could come back so unexpectedly and with such intensity, as if they were yesterday.

I lay on my bed and stared at the ceiling. We had been in the country for less than one day but it had been an emotional roller-coaster already. How on earth was I going to survive nearly four weeks like this? Fortunately, the bliss of being horizontal on a comfy firm mattress, tucked securely into my mosquito net, let me drift quickly off into another world. I'd just have to face each day as I came to it.

Bosco arrived bright and early the next morning and joined us for breakfast. It was going to be a largely administrative day, followed by a visit to my sister-in-law Apollonie in the evening. Administrative things sound boring, but I was just looking forward to being out and about in Kigali, meeting people, checking out what was familiar and what was new, wondering if I might bump into someone I knew. And anyway, these would be 'safe' tasks, no demands on my emotions. I didn't feel ready to start facing the horrors again. But would I ever?

First stop was the office for *Gacaca* – the community courts – to apply for our passes allowing us to attend. The *Gacaca* for the area of Butare where Charles had been staying was due to happen in April, and it would be crucial for us to be there. Charles' name had been added to a list of cases to be examined so we were hoping that some initial enquiries might already have taken place. The plan was to head down to Butare very soon to begin our search, but it would be pointless to go without *Gacaca* passes.

The office was large and unassuming: a concrete floor and whitewashed walls turning dustier and browner towards the floor; a few faded posters on the walls; and four very large desks spread around the edges leaving enough room to dance an eightsome reel in the middle! There were piles of papers and files on most of the desks, and a set of shelves in the corner overflowing with box-files, ring-binders and more piles of yellowing, dusty papers. Two of the desks were empty, and behind the other two sat a couple of employees, chatting.

On their first visit here back in January, the crew had spoken with a very helpful official responsible for registering the passes. But on every subsequent visit they made they were told he was on holiday. Once again, today he was 'on holiday'. In times past I would have found this really frustrating, and it might have led to us being told to come back in two weeks or more. But fortunately today there was someone else who was willing to deal with our request. He examined our documents slowly and deliberately, then copied the information meticulously into his big black book, all neatly lined by hand into rows and columns. We had brought stacks of passport photos and made umpteen photocopies of various bits of our passports before coming, but inevitably there were some bits found to be missing and so we were despatched off a few hundred metres down the road to get more copies.

The tiny photocopy/telephone/fax kiosk at the side of the road seemed to be doing a roaring trade, though it was beyond me how they kept their machines working. Clouds of reddish-brown dust were blown up by every passing vehicle and dust swirled and settled everywhere, despite the array of pieces of plastic and cloth draped over the machines to protect them. As we stood waiting for our photocopies the light outside suddenly began to disappear as thick black clouds obscured the sun. Only by jogging back up the road did we make it safely inside the office again as huge drops of rain began cascading down. And we just made it inside the office as the staff were about to leave and lock up for lunch. However, to my surprise the man dealing with our requests offered to stay and complete our applications before taking his lunch break. Maybe even that was preferable to going outside and getting soaked to the skin in seconds!

We presented our photocopies. More meticulous checking. More columns to fill up in the black book. But finally he declared our paperwork to be in order. So, *Gacaca* passes ready? Well, no, not quite yet. They still needed to be officially signed, and the person who would have to sign them was, unfortunately, not in the office.

'But he'll be in later today,' we were assured, 'so if you come back tomorrow they will definitely be ready for you.' Fair enough. Anyway, this was just our first day, so I couldn't expect everything to run completely smoothly. We'd planned to have our first few days in Kigali for this very reason, so if we could get away with only one day's delay we'd be doing quite well.

Maybe I should have been itching to get going and

frustrated by any delay to our plans? Our time was short and we had a lot to pack into it. But deep down I suppose I was relieved by any delay if it gave me a little more time before I had to face the facts. I wouldn't have much stalling time, though. My sister-in-law, Apollonie, had written to me just before I left the UK and told me that she had some fresh news about Charles' circumstances. We had arranged to visit her and the family this evening. Of course I was looking forward to seeing my in-laws again but being with them was always a painful reminder of the past, even when the past was never mentioned. But this time it would be the focus of our conversation – with new information brought to light. The facts would have to be faced.

I had never known much about the circumstances surrounding Charles' death. When the genocide had begun in April 1994 I had been in Kenya on a brief holiday, joining my sister Sue from Scotland, but leaving Charles behind in Rwanda. Of course, like everyone else I had had no idea what was brewing. The news of the Rwandan President's death first reached me via a doctor in Mombassa, on Kenya's idyllic coast. I'd called him out to our hotel room on the sea front to examine Sue, who had suddenly become very ill with acute food poisoning and dehydration (as we later discovered). With the oppressive heat and without access to water we could be sure was boiled, I was terrified that she was slipping away from me. In fact, Sue got over the worst reassuringly quickly, but we were then both left glued to the BBC World Service on my little short-wave radio, stunned speechless by the unfolding news of murders and massacres, spreading, it seemed, by the minute throughout the tiny country of Rwanda.

I was desperate to get back to Nairobi to make contact with Charles. We had no phone at home, nor where Charles had been temporarily staying, but surely I'd be able to speak to my sister-in-law, Apollonie, or other friends in Kigali and find out exactly what was going on? We were due to take the overnight train back to Nairobi that night but, as if life had not become complicated enough, there had been a derailment on the only railway line between Mombassa and Nairobi and it was likely to be a few days before the trains would run again. We tried the airport but, with hundreds of other tourists stranded as we were, the planes were now all booked up.

I was stranded in Mombassa, with an amazingly selfless but very unwell sister, desperate for news of my husband and friends back home in Rwanda. Eventually I made contact with another tourist family in our hotel who were hiring a vehicle to drive back to Nairobi over a day and a night through one of Kenya's amazing wildlife parks, and they kindly agreed to take us with them.

For the few days we spent in Nairobi, Sue rested to regain her strength and I rushed around madly from British to Belgian and back to British Embassy, frantically trying to persuade some official to include Charles in their military rescue efforts in Rwanda. Plane loads of expatriates and a few Rwandans were being rapidly evacuated but Charles would have no way of getting safely to the airport, past the numerous makeshift barriers all along the roads, manned by drunken, red-eyed machete-wielding and club-swinging militia. The military would have to go and search for him, but neither embassy was prepared to take the risk of jeopardising the whole rescue effort by searching out one single individual. I was desperate, but the situation seemed utterly hopeless.

In between times I was spending literally hours on the phone trying, almost always unsuccessfully, to make contact with friends in Rwanda. Was it the dire Kenyan telephone system or had everyone fled from their homes? And in every spare minute I listened with incredulity and growing horror to the news bulletin descriptions of the bloody mayhem spreading throughout the country.

Colleagues evacuated from Gahini brought some bits of

news: Anatolie, my good friend and close colleague for over four years was among the first to be brutally murdered in our village. I can hardly describe how sickened I was to learn of her death, and of the equally senseless attack on her three-year-old daughter, Liliose. But no one could give me any news of Charles. In the end Sue and I came back to the UK and the long wait for news began.

Over the following months a number of rumours began to reach me bringing snippets of information – often quite contradictory – as to what might have happened to him. He had been with friends in Butare and they were killed but he wasn't. He was killed in Butare Cathedral. He had been seen in the marketplace. He had taken a room at Butare diocesan guest-house and then disappeared. At each report my hopes were raised or dashed. At one minute I would fantasise about his rescue and the welcome he would be given on arrival at Edinburgh Airport. The next I looked at mutilated bodies on the TV reports and imagined that one of them might be his. I dreamed of going back to Rwanda and of our emotional reunion. And then I feared that such an emotional reunion might never be – that he might walk away from me as he had done through our marriage difficulties of the preceding months.

Was I still a wife, a community health worker, a Tearfund employee who would soon be returning to life in Rwanda to pick up the pieces? Or was I now a widow, with no home, no job and a completely uncertain future? The months of confusion and not knowing were almost unbearable. It was as if time had stood still. Even knowing the worst imaginable would be better than this lostness. I had to get back to find out what I could.

Tearfund booked my flight for the end of September. The genocide had ended in July 1994, but the country was still utterly devastated. Of the eight million population it was estimated that some eight hundred thousand to one million had been slaughtered, and a further two million had fled the country and were now living as refugees in neighbouring Tanzania and Zaire. Most of the government and army had also fled the country and tens of thousands of Rwandans who had been living in exile for over thirty years had come back into the country. In such a chaotic situation how would it ever be possible to track down one single individual?

Then, as now, it was my sister-in-law, Apollonie, who was my first port of call and who was able to provide the information to start us on our quest. Then, as now, we would have to go to the Diocese of Butare from where the rumours had originated, in the hope that there might be someone left around who was witness to Charles' last days.

In 1994 the late Bishop of Butare was still living in his diocesan house with his wife. As head of the church in that area and responsible for the diocesan guest-house in which Charles was said to have been staying, surely he would know what had happened? I remember at the time being singularly unimpressed by the man when we visited him. He seemed uncomfortable in our presence, showed no compassion towards us, though as grieving relatives we had come to investigate the death of our loved one, and seemed more concerned to talk about how many of his things he had lost during the genocide – while sitting in his comfortable armchair in a room packed full of furniture. Given the enormous loss of life all around and the abject poverty most survivors now lived in, his attitude seemed at the time unbelievably self-centred.

He told us what he knew – namely that Charles had indeed taken a room at the guest-house, that friends living in the diocese had regularly invited him for meals, but that a few days later some soldiers had come to the guest-house and taken Charles away. Few other details were mentioned, nor any names of others around at the time. It seemed the Bishop and his wife were the only people left in the diocese who had also been there during the genocide.

I had to assume, since there had been neither sight nor

sound of Charles anywhere in this tiny close-knit country for six months, that he was dead. But there was no way of knowing who had taken him, where they had taken him to or what had happened to him. We had to leave with huge unanswered questions. For nearly ten years I then lived with these great holes in my understanding of what had happened to Charles. I had had to get used to the fact that I'd never know any more.

A few days before returning to Rwanda in 2004 I had received a letter from Apollonie with new information. She had met a first-hand witness, Jeannette, who not only had been with Charles during his last days, but also had news of a diocesan pastor, whom she suspected may have had a part to play in Charles' disappearance. Might this be a clue to finding some of the missing pieces of the jigsaw? It was a major shift in my thinking to get my head around the fact that I actually might find the information I was looking for. I know this was the whole purpose of our planned visit, but having lived for so many years with not knowing, I was finding it really difficult to grasp the possibility of getting to the bottom of Charles' murder.

Visiting Apollonie that evening a name came up which we were to hear again and again over the course of our time in Rwanda. The man was a pastor in Butare Diocese, the diocesan secretary for Butare, as Charles had been for Gahini, a senior pastor living in one of the three houses allocated for pastors in the diocesan compound. His name was Kabalira.

Apollonie also spoke of the meeting she had had with Jeannette, who, with her late husband pastor Philip, had also been living in the diocesan compound at the time. They had apparently shown great kindness to Charles in his last days, sharing their meals and spending their days with him. They must have been the 'friends' of whom the late Bishop had spoken ten years previously.

Throughout the evening Apollonie talked at length of the

conversation she had had with Jeannette and of her visit to Kabalira in prison. Their two accounts of the events leading up to Charles' disappearance differed considerably, and there was no doubting whose version Apollonie was more inclined to believe. But it was not enough for me to hear all this information second hand. I'd have to meet Jeannette and Kabalira and hear for myself.

I came away from the evening with Apollonie and Faustin apprehensive and confused, thoughts spinning around in my head. Hearing all the talk of the events of 1994 and feeling the anger in Apollonie's voice brought the memories all back to me so vividly. But it brought up a question for me. Apart from these two contacts I had the impression that Apollonie had done nothing else to investigate Charles' death. What about her late father and stepmother – had she investigated their deaths? It seemed that most people were not asking questions about the terrible deaths of their families and friends. Why not? I wondered. Did they, like me, have little hope of finding anything out? But with the coming of the *Gacaca* was this not now the time to find out?

The visit also raised new issues for me. Here was someone – Jeannette – who had been with Charles in his last days. What might she be able to tell me of his state of mind, his thoughts, his fears, his regrets, his hopes? Things had not been good between us when I'd gone off to Kenya and in the months that had followed I had often wondered about what he might have been thinking in the few weeks leading up to his death. Did he regret not coming to Kenya with me as I had pleaded with him to do? Or did he regret ever marrying me in the first place? Was he hoping to get through this crisis so we could try again to patch up our marriage, or was he hoping he'd never have to see me again? Perhaps he would have spoken with Jeannette and she might be able to tell me.

It felt incredibly important to see Jeannette; she was probably the last person who had given Charles some kindness and care. But to discuss such intensely personal matters with Jeannette in front of the camera? To have our 'dirty washing' made completely public to whoever would watch this documentary? No. I decided I'd ask them to film the 'official' conversation about what actually happened over those last days, but then insist on some time alone with Jeannette to talk of more private issues.

Actually, I was beginning to regret having the camera crew around. It had been extremely hard work with Apollonie, trying to focus and be natural in such a crucial conversation, while aware of movement and whispers elsewhere in the room. There were times when my Kinyarwandan was decidedly rusty and I was struggling to express myself, and I knew that Bosco our translator would be just itching to help me out! But he wasn't part of the set, so I couldn't suddenly just turn and talk to him.

However, it didn't end there. It wasn't particularly late when we left Apollonie's and returned to the guest-house, so the crew asked if I would be prepared to do another little bit of filming. Just a short conversation with Sue over a cup of tea, a bit of a resume of the day and a run-down of the plans from here. If that was what they wanted, I said I'd do my best – although what I really wanted at this point was to hide away and process the day in my own way. But sitting under the harsh neon light on the communal veranda outside the dining room, slapping at the mosquitoes on my unprotected ankles, feeling extremely self-conscious as other guests tried not to disturb us (or watched from a distance!), I was most definitely not able to be myself – and the conversation was a bit of a disaster. I wouldn't have been here at this point were it not for the film crew. And they had already gathered so much information and made key contacts, without which I could do very little. But how was I going to cope for three weeks with this constant intrusion on my most personal and private life? I was beginning to wonder if I might have made an enormous mistake in agreeing to come.

3

Tensions in the Team

'These are your *Gacaca* passes – but wait a moment. There is someone here who, er, who wants to help you.'

It was first thing on Wednesday morning, and Sue, Phil and I were back in the *Gacaca* offices. To our great relief (and surprise) our *Gacaca* passes were ready and waiting for us. It seemed all too good to be true. And maybe it was… But why this request to wait?

We were invited to follow the administrator up another echoing concrete staircase and along more dark corridors, waiting while he paused outside a door, then knocked. No reply. Maybe the person who had wanted to 'help' us had thought better of it. But undeterred he knocked on another door, this time with success, and we were ushered inside.

It was a small office, but with the extra chair brought in there was just room enough for the four of us to sit down. I had no idea what this was all about and was feeling very glad that I was not on my own. Introductions were brief. This gentleman had been one of the local councillors in the Gahini area and now seemed to have some responsibility for the *Gacaca* in that area. His questions to me were unusually direct. What was my purpose here in Rwanda – to investigate the death of my husband or to make a documentary? For me there was no doubt that the documentary was of secondary importance, but he didn't seem entirely satisfied with my response. So if I was here to investigate my husband's death then why was I going to Gahini since Charles had not been in Gahini when he was taken? I was a bit taken aback by this questioning, and by how much he seemed to know, but it wasn't hard to answer. I pointed out that having lived in Gahini for a number of years I still had very good friends there and was really looking forward to seeing them again. And there was another reason. My close friend and colleague, Anatolie, had been murdered in Gahini and I was hoping to attend the Gahini *Gacaca* to find out what exactly had happened to her. I was also hoping that someone might give me some ideas where to begin looking for her only surviving child, Liliose, whom I hadn't seen since visiting her in the refugee camps in Tanzania ten years previously.

The questioning continued. What had been my relationship with the ex-administrator of the hospital and what did I know of his involvement in the genocide? Would I be prepared to give evidence in his trial? What could I tell him about the murder of the former school headmaster in 1990 – did I know who was responsible? Now I was really beginning to get anxious. We had been told this man wanted to help us in our quest, but he seemed only intent on hammering me with questions. I had nothing to hide, but then I had little to offer either. In 1990, though deeply shocked by the violent death of a good man, I was naive and ignorant of the political tensions of the time. And in 1994 I wasn't in Gahini when the genocide happened, so all I knew were snippets of information I'd heard second or third hand. But I wondered if he was assessing whether he might recommend I be called to give evidence at the Gahini *Gacaca* – as a British former colleague of mine had been just a few days previously.

I had been so looking forward to going to Gahini – but not if it was now going to mean facing an interrogation like this one. But then his manner changed. One of his colleagues had been living in Gahini at the same time as me, he explained, and knew of our situation – that women had been spreading malicious rumours about problems in our marriage relationship. 'You must hate Rwandans,' he said with a tone of sympathy and sadness. Again I was taken aback by how much he knew about us, and this time by his apparent compassion. But how could I put all Rwandans in the same basket and hate them all, I replied, when some of the most courageous, compassionate and generous people I know are Rwandan? He asked what I been able to discover about the circumstances leading to Charles' death and so I told him all I knew, while he listened intently. I was then invited to write the details I had just told him in his book – a large black hard-backed notebook into which many people before me had hand-written their stories. I noticed my hand was shaking as I wrote. I also added details about Anatolie's death, and began to ask him if he knew anything about her. But clearly he had already extracted from us whatever information he was looking for and Anatolie was of no interest to him.

There was a colleague in Butare, he said, who would be glad to help us. He gave us his name and phone number. 'But the *Gacaca* in Butare won't be happening in April,' he added, with his hand on the door handle. 'It might be in June, but we're not sure yet.' This news came as a blow. We had been pinning a lot of importance on the Butare *Gacaca* as a key opportunity to hear witness testimonies and ask questions about the circumstances surrounding Charles' disappearance. But at the same time the delay didn't surprise me one little bit. This was life in Rwanda. Events often had to be postponed at very short notice – announcements made on the radio or passed by word of mouth. Sometimes a national holiday would be announced on the radio in the early morning – but children would turn up at school, having walked miles to get there, only to find the place closed. The word had not reached them in time.

I remembered in 1995 my sister-in-law Apollonie writing to me to say that a funeral – the reburying of excavated bones amongst which might well have been Charles' – would be taking place in Butare on a date in October just a couple of weeks later. On the strength of her letter I went out immediately and bought a plane ticket to Rwanda for a week. But when I told her I was coming she was concerned in case the funeral might not actually happen during my short visit to Rwanda. Although it would be a major national event attended by thousands, with political and church leaders from all over the country, it was still not known exactly when it would happen. I think the date was finally agreed only two or three days before the actual event.

The postponement of the Butare *Gacaca* was frustrating, but my attitude was to shrug my shoulders. I didn't realise how very disappointing this announcement would be to the crew, or how annoyed they would be at me for my seeming indifference. I guess I had been doing a lot of my thinking and processing internally instead of expressing my thoughts clearly and openly, and this led to miscommunication and misunderstanding.

Anyway, as we left the *Gacaca* building the comments focussed more on the helpfulness of both the men we had talked to there – and it was true, they had been sympathetic to our situation and had given us useful information. But something deep in my gut felt very uncomfortable about the conversation that had just taken place. I can be so gullible at times, and without thinking I had ended up telling this councillor all the details of my story. But had that been wise? Could I trust him or might he have a hidden agenda? I could think of no reason why the information I had given him could in any way backfire, either on me or on other friends I had mentioned. But the old nagging doubts and suspicions were coming back to me again. Is there *anyone* here who can be trusted? I had been introduced to this man as someone who 'could help us', but really he wanted to pick my brains about what I knew about Gahini, in particular about the former hospital administrator and the death of the headmaster. It shocked me to think how willingly I had gone to meet this 'helpful' person when all the time he might have had another motive of which I knew nothing. Maybe I was reading too much into it, but it made me think how easily Charles and the diocesan staff might have been taken in by the military officials who had come for Charles in 1994. If they said he was being taken away for questioning, why doubt it? Perhaps they were charming and not nasty or threatening. How easy to be taken in and go along with it. How utterly impossible to know who to trust.

I'm sure Sue and Phil thought I was a bit paranoid, though they kindly didn't say so! But then unless you've lived through a situation where trust has totally broken down and truth has been turned on its head, how can you be expected to understand or to feel the malaise deep down inside? It was intensely frustrating trying to put these feelings across to enable the others to get inside what I was experiencing, but as the days turned to weeks in the country, each person with me came to feel for themselves something of this disturbing malaise and suspicion.

It would be so good to get back home to Gahini the next day. I had friends there who were straight as a plank and who had no hidden agendas with me. Gahini was familiar to me so maybe I'd feel more myself there. In fact, with our *Gacaca* passes safely tucked away, and as there wasn't much left to do in Kigali at this point, could we not just go *now* to Gahini? But there was one other person to see in Kigali before we left. After numerous attempts to make contact with the Archbishop, we had finally arranged to meet up briefly that afternoon. So I'd have to be patient just a little longer.

Archbishop Kolini had been extremely helpful already in smoothing the way for us. With the Archbishop of the Episcopal Church in Rwanda giving his full support to their investigations, the crew had been able to make contacts and open doors perhaps more quickly and easily than would otherwise have been possible. I had heard many good reports

of him and I really wanted to meet him to say thank you. But
he was an extremely busy man, difficult even to track down
on his mobile phone. Today, however, we had success. He
would be at a meeting in the afternoon at Kigali Diocese, he
told us, and would be delighted to see us briefly to say hello.

Over lunch, as we sat for ages waiting for our goat or
tilapia brochettes to appear, I became increasingly conscious
of an awkwardness and tension in the atmosphere. I hate
conflict and always assume somehow I'm in the wrong, so
I'm useless at confronting the silence to find out what's the
problem. Often, of course, the atmosphere has nothing
whatsoever to do with me anyway! But this time it did. It
turned out that some of the team were feeling annoyed over
how I had been responding to the filming. They felt I was
not being real enough on camera – 'performing' when being
filmed, then relaxing and talking about my real feelings
after. I was playing safe, being very guarded in what I said
on film while it was obvious to them that at times my real
feelings were quite different. Ouch! That hurt. I was taken
aback, not just by what was being said, but by what I felt to
be anger behind the words. And then, as I tried to respond to
the accusations, I began to feel really indignant. I guessed
the incidents they were referring to were that awkward
conversation with Sue in the evening after our visit to
Apollonie's house, and my insistence that the crucial part of
my conversation with Jeanette to find out about Charles
should be in private without the camera. I suppose the hurt
was because I felt that my situation had not really been
understood. Yes, they were probably right that I was holding
back when on camera. But I was very conscious of what it
was acceptable to say publicly here and what it was not. The
frankness with which we were used to speaking in the West
is generally not at all acceptable in a Rwandan context. I
was finding it strange to be straddling the two cultures this
time. Usually when in Rwanda I would have been primarily
with Rwandans and over the years had probably

subconsciously taken on board some of the cultural nuances. But this time, although I was back on familiar territory in Rwanda, I was also closeted within that, in a British huddle. As a result I felt kind of disorientated. How should I respond? And then there were just the normal adjustments of being back with all the extremes of emotional response evoked in me. We had been in the country for less than two days and it was my first time back after five years. I had a lot to take in, just of the sounds, smells, sights and memories of normal life around me. I wasn't ready to put my full concentration into the quest ahead of us. But time was very short. I hadn't had the luxury of taking a few days to acclimatise before starting the real work.

In the end, we agreed that they should be allowed to film anything – including my conversation with Jeannette – and that I should express openly my responses and impressions, on the understanding that if I later decided there were things I really did not want to be part of the documentary, then they could be taken out. Had I known at that stage the devastating news Jeannette was soon to share with me I might have been more cautious in giving my agreement to film *anything*.

Meeting the Archbishop that afternoon was an experience I'll never forget. We had been told he was deeply ensconced in some high-powered bishops' meeting so we were standing around in Kigali Diocese car park, chatting animatedly with some old friends I'd bumped into, when suddenly I became aware of someone else who had quietly joined us.

Archbishop Kolini greeted me warmly with the traditional Rwandan two-sided hug, but then instead of pulling back to shake hands as would be normal, he held onto me in a tight embrace, his gentle words flowing into prayer for me as he stroked my shoulder. Slowly, and full of compassion, with his fatherly arms holding me firmly, he talked to God of the pain I had suffered through the genocide and of the traumatic journey ahead of me over these next weeks. And as he prayed my tears trickled down the shoulder of his jacket. In a country where almost every person has faced unspeakable loss and trauma it was hard for me to give weight to my own suffering because it seemed so minimal compared to others. But here was someone acknowledging *my* pain and grief with such tenderness and pastoral care, it completely overwhelmed me. He couldn't stay long. The bishops were waiting for him back in the meeting. But I will never forget the kindness he showed me in these brief few minutes.

The view from the road as it winds along the edge of Lake Muhazi towards Gahini and on beyond to Uganda is stunning at any time of day, but in the early evening as the setting sun turns the sky to a deep orange-red that joins as a continuum with the great expanse of the lake, it is just breathtaking. As we rounded the last corner the sign to Gahini came into view, pointing steeply uphill to the right, onto a red-brown muddy road. Home at last! Ah, but not quite yet. The minibus was slowing down and turning off to the left instead of up the hill to the right. For the first time in my life, though right on the doorstep of my 'home' village, I would not actually be staying there.

We were booked into the diocesan guest-house – the Seeds of Peace. Built after the genocide it has been the subject of deep resentment for many of the parishioners of Gahini Diocese, struggling for survival in abject poverty. Why waste precious money on luxurious accommodation for rich Rwandans and foreign tourists when so many in the area were suffering? I felt embarrassed to be staying there. But on the other hand it is a stunningly beautiful setting. Right on the edge of the lake, flanked by an expanse of lush green lawn, three white round huts with thatched roofs each open out onto their own spacious balcony overlooking papaya trees and bougainvillea, down to the lake and beyond. The huts were simply but adequately furnished, each with two bedrooms, a tiny kitchen area, a shower room and a large sitting/dining area.

We arrived to find one hut had been double-booked, causing a flurry of confusion in the small group of Rwandan staff. But with Ray and Bosco nobly agreeing to sleep on extra mattresses on the sitting room floor all six of us would manage to squeeze into one hut for the first night.

By the time we'd sorted ourselves out it was too late to walk up into the village that evening, so we ordered some food and made plans for the next day.

Since leaving Rwanda in 1994 I had been back a few times to visit and had kept in regular contact with friends like John and Gemima and their children, the family I'd lived with at the beginning of my time in Rwanda. Over the years I had closely followed the ups and downs in their lives, constantly humbled by their faith, courage and cheerfulness in the face of terrible struggles and hardship. I had actually only spent six weeks living at John and Gemima's house, but they've included me as part of their family ever since. I went to live with them when I was new, vulnerable and dependent. They looked after me, taught me the language and the customs, laughed with me at my strange ways, organised and hosted our wedding, cried with me in my pain in later years and prayed for me from before I even met them. We shared so much of our lives together. And now, very soon, I was going to see them again.

John and Gemima now lived in a house by the side of the road near the marketplace, quite far through the sprawling village of Gahini. But this was not their original family home. During the genocide of 1994, Gahini and much of the eastern side of Rwanda had virtually emptied out, great swathes of the population fleeing south to neighbouring Tanzania in fear of the invading Rwandan Patriotic Army (RPA). The RPA, made up of Tutsi refugees who had fled to Uganda some thirty years previously and many disaffected, disillusioned Hutus from Rwanda, crossed the border in north-eastern Rwanda and swept south and west seeking to stop the mass slaughter. Terrified of reprisals, guilty and innocent alike had fled Gahini and the surrounding areas in eastern Rwanda in their tens of thousands, leaving very few behind. Following the RPA's arrival from the north, however, came many thousands more Rwandans, desperate to return to their homeland after thirty years as refugees in Uganda. Many of these newcomers had previously lived in this area and saw it as their right to reclaim their land and property again. Others simply took over any empty property around, and once again the rural eastern edge of Rwanda was densely populated.

One of these families had taken over John and Gemima's home – and they had no intention of leaving. When John and Gemima returned to Gahini, after two-and-a-half years in the refugee camps in Tanzania, they had to proceed extremely cautiously. Theoretically they had the right to appeal to the legal system to regain possession of their own house, but that carried the risk of reprisal attacks and even killings. Not being people who insisted on their rights or ever made a fuss, they found a derelict, run-down property and moved in there temporarily. It had holes in the iron-sheeting roof where the rain came in, and there were no windows or proper door – but still they survived there for a year. Over these months they slowly built a relationship with the occupiers of their own house, and eventually it was vacated, enabling them to move back in. Of course it was in a poor state of repair now, and very few of their possessions were left. Some of their furniture had been spotted in other people's houses locally, but they had no desire to cause trouble by reclaiming it. Through all of this they uttered not one word of complaint. They were simply delighted to be back in their own home again, and their focus was constantly on God, whom they praised for looking after them and providing for them. Their joy at being back home, however, was short-lived. A year later, after working hard to clean up and renovate their house, the government decided to issue a law stating that it was now illegal to live away from the edges of the main roads.

Rwanda is a mainly rural economy, and the countryside is full of tiny homesteads dotted all over the hills and valleys. To insist that everyone should live along the sides of the roads would be extremely disruptive for many people. But the idea seemed to be to encourage both Hutu and Tutsi to live close to each other in an attempt to break down the suspicion and hostility that had become so much worse after the genocide. People would have to find their own accommodation and there would be no compensation for the properties they were forced to vacate. Rows of new houses were being built along the sides of the roads, but these would be woefully inadequate for the huge numbers of people now compelled to leave the countryside.

John and Gemima's house was some distance from the road, reached only by narrow paths winding through their banana patches and small fields. So, once again, they would have to move. The land would still belong to them, so they would still be able to cultivate their crops, but it was now a long walk to reach the fields, and not living nearby left it open and vulnerable to theft, especially of their valuable sticks of bananas. Eventually they found an old run-down mud house right on the main dirt road through Gahini market area, and were able to transfer the few movable items from their own place – the iron-sheeting for the roof and some doors and window-frames. But it was extremely basic. The house they had built for themselves in the refugee camp in Tanzania was more substantial than this miserable shack. This was now their fourth move in less than four years and each time the property they moved into was worse than the one they had left. Since coming back to Rwanda they had not been able to get any work – despite being experienced and capable – probably because of prejudice against returning refugees. And yet despite all that they remained, as ever, undaunted, trusting in God, and grateful beyond belief for what they still had.

Ironically, some years after this last move, the government revoked the law of living along the roadside as it was found to be unworkable. But by this time their original home was in ruins and they had invested sacrificially in repairing their new one. I had seen their 'new' home soon after they had moved in, on my last visit to Rwanda, so I was looking forward to seeing how it had changed. But much more than that I was looking forward to seeing the family again. Their sixth child, my goddaughter Suzanne, was just little last time I saw her. Would she remember or recognise me? I had passed on messages to say I was coming but would they have got through?

After another delicious breakfast of fresh fruit, omelettes, bread and coffee sitting on the balcony watching the occasional dug-out canoe drifting slowly past on the still waters of Lake Muhazi, we set off on the climb up the hill to Gahini. To get to John and Gemima's house we'd have to go right through the heart of the village, skirting the edge of the hospital and rehabilitation centre, past the primary and secondary schools, past the large, red-brick church, and past a row of small mud shops with a meagre supply of basic commodities and locally-brewed alcohol. I could picture it all in my mind. And all along the way we'd be accompanied by groups of laughing, skipping children all fascinated by the *bazungu* in their midst.

Sue and I were walking together, excitedly picking out familiar sights. The crew followed behind, although Phil displayed amazing energy, at times running up the hill ahead of us to get a shot of us puffing and panting, the lake glistening way down below. As we rounded the corner at the top of the hill and the schools and church came into sight I could feel my anticipation rising. It was so good to be back!

Suddenly, from among a crowd of brightly clad women sitting on concrete benches outside a classroom came a squeal I recognised immediately.

'Rezire!'[1] shrieked the voice, bursting with excitement.

'Gemima!' I yelled back. 'Gemima, weh!' As I began to run towards the source of the voice from behind the hedge I could see Gemima running over the grass towards us. I just couldn't get there fast enough! The schoolchildren who had been surrounding us scattered as I charged through their midst, almost falling on top of Gemima as we threw our arms around each other, hugging tightly and crying with excitement. A few seconds later, as the kids crowded around jostling and giggling at us, I suddenly became aware, out of the corner of my eye, of one child clad in a bright blue school uniform dress crashing through them towards us like a bullet. The next moment there were two little arms squeezing tightly around my neck and two little legs wrapped around my waist. Suzanne had certainly not forgotten who I was!

The whole of that day and the next were spent in a whirlwind of visiting, chatting and catching up. We talked for some time with Manwelli, who was still working as a gardener in the house next to where Charles and I had lived. A more gentle, patient, compassionate man you could never meet. We visited Vasta, Gemima's elderly mum and my adopted granny, who brought up her family single-handedly and now cares for her nine orphaned grandchildren and two great-grandchildren. One of her grandsons, my godson Jacques, now a good-looking teenager but still with the same cheeky glint in his eye I remembered from when he was three, took me proudly to see his goats. I had given him a goat as a present following my last visit, as a way of supplementing the meagre family income. I knew it had reproduced and they'd been able to sell a few kids over the years. But as he opened the door to a dark little shed and my eyes adjusted to the total absence of sunlight I was shocked to see about fifteen goats of various sizes all squashed in together. The shed was very mucky and small, but the goats looked healthy enough, and he assured me he took them out for long periods every day to find grass.

A few minutes later, as we sat huddled on low benches in Vasta's sitting room, chatting and reminiscing over old faded photos in a much-travelled, precious photo album, there was a kind of surreal moment. The mobile phone rang and Ray went outside to answer. It was Sylvie from Tearfund's media department in London. Fergal Keane, the BBC's Africa correspondent, for whom I have enormous respect, was in Rwanda for the commemorations of the tenth anniversary of the genocide and would like to interview me. Could I call to arrange it please?

Vasta's family knew little about the BBC or Fergal Keane, but they were fascinated by Ray's mobile phone. So, later we arranged to call Vasta's grandson Jean-Pierre, a student in Kigali (who had borrowed a friend's phone for the occasion), to give her her first opportunity in her eighty-something years to talk on the phone! I tell you, watching the expressions on Vasta's face as I held the phone to her ear and she heard his voice at the other end had us all nearly weeping with laughter. Mobile phones had opened up communications even in rural Rwanda in a way unthinkable just a few years ago.

We visited others in their homes along the way and chatted to old friends we met on the road, but we couldn't stay anywhere long as we had been invited to lunch at John and Gemima's. At each place we stopped on the way I mentioned Anatolie's orphaned daughter, Liliose, hoping someone might have some suggestions of how to find her, but everyone seemed quite vague on the subject. By the time we reached their house, quite late, there were large steaming bowls of rice, beans, fried bananas and peanut sauce with aubergines waiting for us. Wonderful! There was so much to catch up on with them, and here, of all places, I found it hard to have so many other *bazungu* with me. I wanted to talk with them about ordinary things in life, the family, their work possibilities, how their house was progressing, and the news from around in the village. But I felt self-conscious with the others around and having to translate all the time. And I was there with an agenda – to focus on our mission of finding Charles' killers – so general chat was brief and our conversation was limited. Had they heard anything through the grapevine about who might have been responsible for Charles' death? What, if anything, did they know about Pastor Kabalira? How did they cope with knowing that church leaders were implicated in the genocide?

I tried to share with them the news Apollonie had given me about Charles, but all these deeply personal, private issues are simply not talked about in a group setting so I felt awkward and they were very guarded in their responses. It was not easy. If only I could have sent the other *bazungu* away for the rest of the day and just relaxed with the family! Well, I'd just have to be patient. Maybe that chance would come another time. Meanwhile we had to move on.

So far, all these visits had been within reasonable walking distance from each other, but there was a good friend I wanted to visit who lived miles up the road right into the countryside. We wouldn't have time to walk there, so John had arranged for all of us to go as passengers on bicycles – camera equipment and all! I was excited to be going out into the wide open spaces again. Anatolie and I used to drive out this road two or three times every week, whether to a distant mobile health clinic, to do a home visit with our health workers or for an AIDS prevention teaching session at one of the primary schools. I loved that side of the work; I loved the fresh air and freedom of being out in the countryside, and I loved the chats Anatolie and I would have as we travelled. All these feelings came rushing back as we cycled along, so real, almost tangible, and yet agonisingly unreachable. It would never again be as it had been before. Anatolie was dead. She had been one of the first to be attacked when the killing began in Gahini.

I remembered hearing about her death while I was in Kenya on that fateful brief 'holiday'. In between numerous phone calls and frantic visits to embassies to try and make contact with Charles to enable his evacuation from Rwanda, I also had a few trips to the airport. Some of the expatriate colleagues with whom I had worked in Gahini were arriving in Nairobi and I was desperate for some news of Charles, my 'family' and friends. On one occasion I went to Nairobi's Wilson Airport, where some of my colleagues were arriving on a small plane. Security was relaxed, so I was able to greet them on the tarmac and stand with them as they waited in the queue at passport check.

'What news from Gahini?' I asked, desperate to know what was happening there. I had heard there had been attacks but didn't know who had been killed.

There was an awkward silence as they looked at each other. Clearly there was something they didn't want me to know.

'I have to know,' I said, 'however bad it is. Please tell me.'

A number of people had been killed, but mostly they weren't hospital staff and these short-term volunteers didn't know them. But... but they did know Anatolie. She had been murdered on the day the killings began.

I remember my head reeling. I couldn't take it in. Anatolie. Why Anatolie? She was a good woman. Surely she didn't have an enemy in the world. But she and her husband were from the Tutsi tribe, and when the killers came looking for her husband but didn't find him, they killed her instead. Anatolie's elder daughter, Mireille, had tragically died of malaria in the February of 1994, only two months before the genocide began. So her one remaining child, Liliose, had lost sister, mother and father in the space of two months, and had herself been attacked but survived. So much extreme tragedy in one small life. Now, back in the country, it felt really important for me to find her and make contact again after ten long years. But how would I ever find her?

My 'chauffeur' seemed to be a lively guy, and we chatted a little as he peddled valiantly along the bumpy road.

Everything looked so familiar, the occasional house set back from the road with neatly swept earth road leading up to it, the patch of fir trees, the wild bushes of strong-smelling tiny pink and yellow flowers. Back in Kigali there had been so much new building, but here out in the countryside nothing seemed to have changed.

My attention was pulled in lots of places at once, taking in the sights, sounds and smells, the refreshing whispers of breeze in the hot sun, flitting between the present and the past. Then, a mile or so into the journey, my 'chauffeur' turned to me and asked, 'So have you found Liliose yet?' I nearly fell off the bike! How did he know I was looking for her? Could he read my thoughts?

'Well, no,' I stumbled. 'Not yet. But how did you know I was looking for her?' 'I just heard,' he responded, vaguely. 'You see it was my mum who took her from here to Tanzania. She lived with us in the refugee camp.' Again I nearly fell off the bike. There were six people riding these bikes. I knew nothing about any of them. I could have picked any one of them but for some reason I ended up on this guy's bike with the opportunity for a forty-minute private chat (private, that is, apart from the now permanent fixture of the microphone clipped to my shirt and Phil bumping along a few metres ahead of us, camera in hand). But he knew Liliose!

His mother had taken Liliose into her home after Anatolie was killed and Liliose's father had fled. Then, when the majority of the population of Gahini decided to flee from the advancing Rwandan Patriotic Army, she had taken Liliose with her and her young son, now the strapping teenager riding this bike, and they joined the thousands walking to Tanzania. His mother had since died, but he told me he was pretty sure Liliose was now living with her father's relatives in Gitarama, and he gave me the name of a family friend who might be able to tell us precisely where in Gitarama she was living. This was fantastic news! The original remote possibility I thought we had of tracking her down had suddenly become a strong likelihood. She was alive and well. I felt sure we would find her, somehow.

But elation and devastation always seem to go hand in hand for me in this country, and before we could head to Gitarama I was to hear some devastating and unexpected news about Charles.

4

Charles

The town of Rwamagana lay twenty-five kilometres west of Gahini on the road to Kigali. In the pre-mobile phone era and even before landlines came to Gahini this was the nearest place to come to make a phone call.

We were stopping in Rwamagana on our way back to Kigali, having arranged to meet Jeannette at her home there. It was Jeannette who, with her pastor husband, had been living in Butare Diocese when Charles had fled there during the genocide, and who had provided him with meals and support during what were to be his last days.

This was going to be a tough visit. I didn't know Jeannette at all, but I was hugely grateful to her for showing kindness to Charles in such terrifying circumstances. It would be very moving, as two widows together, to talk over these last experiences of our husbands' lives. But I was also anxious about any news she might have as to Charles' state of mind in his last days, and in particular how he might have felt towards me.

As we drove towards Rwamagana, leaving behind the excitement of the past couple of days in Gahini, my thoughts were racing back over the brief months Charles and I had spent together. How could so much happiness have turned so sad and sour?

The early days of our relationship were exciting. When Charles first came to work in Gahini back in 1990 there was something about him that, for me, made him stand out from the crowd. He was lively, friendly and thoughtful. He lived out his Christian faith in down-to-earth compassion. He had carefully thought-through opinions and could enjoy a good discussion. And he happened to be rather good-looking as well.

Although Rwandan by birth, he had spent many years outside the country, firstly in Uganda where he completed his schooling then teacher training, and then in Kenya where he gained his Bachelor of Divinity, fulfilling a desire of many years to train for the Anglican ministry. With this combination of studies his diocese decided to assign him to the church secondary school in Gahini as the English teacher. Charles was one of the very few Rwandans in the area who spoke fluent English and, being something of an outsider himself, he related well to both the local and the expatriate communities. He was an outgoing, sociable guy, who threw himself into life in the church, the school and the community around.

Charles' future life partner had been decided many years ago. He was to marry a girl from his home village. He didn't talk much about her but was keen that I and a few other friends should meet her, possibly at his ordination in Kigali. Perhaps it was because he was unquestionably spoken for that I was able to relax and enjoy spending time with him without any unspoken agendas. However, when the elusive future partner failed to turn up to his ordination and he discovered she was involved with someone else he was devastated and suddenly his plan was turned on its head. Over the months that followed, our friendship slowly grew. Then, one evening, soon after our first (and only) 'date' – a meal out when we both happened to be in Kigali for the same weekend – he suddenly announced to me that I was the girl he wanted to marry!

Presumably he had decided I was suitable enough – in other words, I was reasonably intelligent, could speak a few languages, could cook well enough and wasn't too bad looking. At least these had been the expectations of his senior schoolboys, written in an exercise they had been given to describe their ideal wife. So I guessed they might also be the average expectations of most young Rwandan men. Well, maybe it was straightforward enough for him, but it certainly wasn't that simple for me. As far as I was concerned we hardly knew each other yet, and that would take time. And there were major questions to consider over a whole load of issues – the challenges of a cross-cultural marriage, an indefinite future in Rwanda, distance from family and bringing up possible offspring far from home, job uncertainty and its financial implications, and much, much more.

Charles was, of course, not oblivious to these issues. He had lived in other countries; he had seen life outside Rwanda and had experienced being separated from his family. So these were issues we discussed openly as we considered a possible future together. But he had never been to Europe so there was a very big part of me he could not identify with. We talked through the challenges that would inevitably arise due to different cultural backgrounds and expectations. Charles graciously saw it as his responsibility to help me understand and fit in. If I bungled up and embarrassed us both by behaving inappropriately, he felt that he could only blame himself for not having explained the cultural nuances to me. But the differences we might be aware of were really only the tip of the iceberg. Neither of us had begun to understand the massive subconscious baggage we would both bring into the relationship from our families, our upbringing, and our cultures. Only in the years after the genocide, when studying culture as part of my degree at All Nations Christian College, and later during years of counselling training, did I discover all sorts of things I so wished I'd known when I was married. But life always seems so much easier with the benefit of hindsight...

The preparations for the wedding all happened in a bit of a whirlwind. There were two events to prepare for – the traditional wedding taking place in Gahini, and the church wedding three days later in Kigali Cathedral. Six of my family had come out to join us for the few weeks before and after – my parents, sisters Sheila and Sue, niece Jo and aunt Elsie – so maybe it was just as well that the majority of the preparations were out of my hands.

My Rwandan 'parents', John and Gemima, were to be hosting the traditional event in their own home, just as if I were their own daughter. This meant a meticulous cleaning of the house and grounds, cementing the mud floor of 'my' bedroom as it was to be used as a meeting place for all the girls who would accompany me, erecting awnings of tarpaulin and banana leaves in the front yard to protect the visitors from the glare of the sun, and absolutely enormous amounts of cooking in their backyard with all the neighbouring women joining in.

It's an odd experience to be at your own wedding and not know what is going to happen next! But this wedding was full of surprises. There were the energetic '*intore*' dancers, traditional male dancers leaping into the air, twirling and tossing their feather head-dresses, bells jangling around their ankles, accompanied by traditional instruments played by members of the Twa tribe. There was the arrival of the cow – a gift given from Charles' family to my family – paraded through the centre of the crowds, inspected by a cow expert who then proceeded, in lively song and dance, to compare its value and beauty to that of the bride! And there was the baptism of John and Gemima's youngest son, Ebenezer. Well, why not! With all their friends there, the place prepared and the food ready, surely it made sense to double up with our wedding!

All this fun and activity was somewhat in contrast with

the more solemn reverence of the cathedral wedding ceremony only three days later. But even this wasn't without its
humour. A Scottish friend, Matthew, who read one of the
readings, was as much if not more photographed and talked
about than we were! The reason? He was wearing his kilt for
the occasion.

But the two moments that brought me to tears then, as
they still do now whenever I watch the video of our wedding,
were the soloists. Even now if I close my eyes I can still hear
the magnificent power and clarity of the voice of my sister
Sheila filling that huge cathedral with Handel's 'How
beautiful are the feet of them that bring the Gospel of peace'
from *The Messiah*. And given all the trauma that was to
come our way in the following months, how prophetic were
the words sung by our blind friend, Barthomeo, accompanying himself on the keyboard – 'God will take care of
you.'

The weeks following the weddings brought no respite
from the busyness. As well as having Charles' teenage
nephew living with us, there was a constant stream of visitors
to our door from near and far, every day after work and all
weekend. This was all part of Rwandan tradition, but I was
finding it very stressful.

I remember one Saturday afternoon as yet another group
of visitors sat chatting and drinking tea in the sitting room, I
retreated to the bedroom and sat in tears on the bed. I was
utterly exhausted and couldn't face any more. After some
time Charles came through to find out where I was. But far
from offering me the sympathy I so longed for he instead
tried to persuade me to dry my eyes and come back through.
I suppose it was embarrassing for him that his wife had left
the visitors for so long.

'A Rwandan wife would not have let him down like this,'
I thought to myself, adding a sense of failure and inadequacy
to my stress and tiredness.

Over the weeks it seemed to me that Charles was changing

and perhaps I was too. Before we were married we would often spend evenings together, sharing a meal and chatting over future plans. Now he was rarely home before 9 p.m. I put it down to work. He was a very conscientious teacher, well liked and respected and I knew he was working very hard. Sometimes in the evenings he would go out visiting friends without coming home first to say he might be late. I struggled with this, and complained about it often, but he didn't see it as a problem. It was a man's prerogative to be independent – and a sign of weakness if he always had to consult with his wife.

'I always dreaded having a nagging wife,' he told me once. My reply was predictably unhelpful. 'But I wouldn't have to nag you if you listened to what I said in the first place!'

Neither of us could understand the other's perspective, and so our positions became increasingly entrenched, while on the surface all seemed well and happy.

It was one evening soon after we had returned from a visit to the UK in the summer of 1993 that things began to go seriously wrong. Charles was out as usual, and I had two of the local Christian women visiting me. After the usual pro-tracted pleasantries over a cup of tea and bananas there was a bit of a pause. One of them shifted nervously in her seat.

'When Pastor² is out all evening,' she ventured, hesita-tingly, 'do you know where he is?' 'Yes, of course,' I replied. 'He's down at the school working. He's got a lot of prepara-tion and marking to do.'

The two women looked gravely at each other. 'Lesley, we really didn't want to have to tell you this, but you are a good friend to us and we don't want to see you hurt so you really need to know.' I looked from one to the other. What on earth were they talking about?

'I'm afraid he's not actually at the school. He spends his evenings at Martine's house – you know, Martine the school secretary.'

It was as though I'd been knifed in the stomach. Charles? Having an affair? When we'd only been married a few months? I was furious with these women. How dare they come and make such accusations! But I was furious with Charles too. Had he been lying to me all the time? I believed them – and I doubted them. Were they among those whom Charles had told me would sidle up to me, pretending to be my friend, and try to destroy our marriage out of jealousy? If so, I hated them. Or were they genuinely concerned for me and gutsy enough to tell me what no one else had dared to do? The tears began to run down my cheeks.

'Don't worry too much,' they advised me. 'I'm afraid this happens to a lot of us, but just be patient and he'll come back to you. I remember when...' And they began talking non-stop of several examples where husbands had been unfaithful, but wives had waited patiently over the years of their husbands sleeping around, and somehow it had all worked out.

'...and remember that one who used to bring his women back and sleep with them in the wife's own bed!' 'Yes, and he'd be drunk and in a terrible mess, but his wife would always clean him up after...'

I was drifting in and out of their comments, stunned by the thought of Charles having an affair and furious by their constant ramblings and insensitivity. Suddenly I needed them out of the house. I needed silence on my own to digest what I'd just heard and work out how to respond when Charles would come home that evening.

Charles, of course, denied it completely and was furious at the women for spreading such malicious gossip. Yes, Martine was a friend of his but nothing more. He was godfather to her child and did his best to support her because as a single mum and of the minority Tutsi tribe, like Charles, she had a hard time in Gahini. Maybe he was right. Over the next few weeks I began to believe him again. Things began to improve between us. There were no more rumours about

Martine; he made an effort to come back earlier in the evenings, and we even occasionally visited friends together. And I tried hard not to nag or criticise him. We had some lovely times. But then the rumours against him would reach my ears again and I didn't know who to trust.

Over the next few months we fluctuated between hostilities and suspicion at some times and a restored relationship and good communication at others. Rwandan friends cautioned patience. 'Be patient' was the standard response to any difficult situation no matter how unjust or personally wounding. But my British friends advised toughness. Don't stand for any messing about. Give him an ultimatum. I was completely confused and desperately lonely, longing for a close friend whom I could trust and share with, and doubting the motives of anyone who offered advice.

Most of the time I felt utterly powerless in a situation way out of my hands. But there were other times when, unhelpfully, my response was to take the moral high ground. I believed the devil had got into him and was poisoning his mind. 'You need to repent before God and he will forgive you,' I would say to him. But not surprisingly this only had the opposite effect of driving him further away from me.

In February 1994 Charles moved out of the house and rented a flat in Rwamagana. The previous month my parents had also separated. By this stage I was not eating much, struggling to cope at work and crying at the slightest provocation. My British colleagues had tried to persuade me to go home, but there was no family home to go to and I feared it might jeopardise any chances of Charles and me getting back together again.

However, I did agree to take a break, and in March asked my sister Sue if she would come to Kenya to join me for a couple of weeks. I needed to get right out of the situation and I felt I would be able to talk with her. She and her husband Cameron had five young children, they were about to go off on holiday, and had just put their house on the market. It was the worst time for her to come. But Cameron's response was, 'Sue, if your sister needs you now, you need to go.'

It took only a few hours of Sue's patient listening and compassion for me to realise how enormously helpful it was to have someone trustworthy to whom I could just pour out my soul. In Rwanda I had had plenty of people ready to advise me but no one I could trust who would just listen. And then I realised that Charles was probably in the same position. He was being told what to do by well-meaning friends and family and blamed for the breakdown in our relationship. But I had played a part in that too, and he had every right to be angry with me. Was there anyone to whom *he* could vent his feelings without being judged or criticised? If talking it out had helped me so much, surely it would help him too.

I phoned his sister, Apollonie, in Kigali. She had been very supportive of me, and as she was the oldest of the siblings, a motherly kind of figure, I was hoping he might see her as someone whom he could trust. I asked if she would go and visit him in Rwamagana.

'Please don't tell him what to do or give him any kind of advice,' I pleaded with her on the phone. 'He's angry with me, and he has every right to be. He needs to be able to express that to someone who'll just listen.' She promised to do her best.

Three days later the genocide began.

It was not until six months later that I was able to make contact again with Apollonie, three months after the genocide had ended. Her own family had been scattered, but miraculously had all survived and were now reunited back in their own home in Kigali.

On my first visit back to Rwanda in October 1994 I went immediately to see them in their home. Eventually I plucked up the courage to ask if she had been able to visit Charles as I had requested. She had. 'And he seemed a different person,' she told me. 'More back to his usual self again.' He apparently was grateful that I had asked her to come, and seemed hopeful that we might be able to work things out between us.

This was like music to my ears and I wept with relief. For six months I had been blaming myself for all that had gone wrong between us, struggling much more with forgiving myself than forgiving him. I had always imagined that he hated me and would never want to see me again. So to hear that in his last known contact he had been more himself, the Charles I used to know, and thinking about us getting together again, meant so much to me. I still loved him, despite all that had happened, and this gave me a spark of hope that perhaps somewhere deep inside he still had a grain of love for me too.

The genocide had come when our relationship was at an all-time low. I had had to cope with the horrors of his murder and that of many good friends, as well as the private pain of a broken, unresolved relationship. The former was very public news, broadcast across the country on TV documentaries, radio and newspaper reports. But the latter was intensely private. Only a few people knew of our relationship problems and I was much too ashamed to talk or write about it.

But now at least I could hold onto the fact that, had things been different, we might well have sorted out our differences. The first year of our marriage had been stormy – but I was beginning to realise that was sometimes true for other couples too. So instead of seeing the marriage as a complete failure, I could tell myself that this was a normal hiccup and given time we would have been fine.

Over the next ten years I lived with these thoughts, never quite knowing but always hoping, wanting to believe the best. But now, on our way to Rwamagana, my illusions were about to be shattered.

The rain had eased off a little by the time the minibus drew up outside the huge red-brick Catholic cathedral just off the main road. We had arranged to meet Jeannette here so she could take us to her house, but there was no sign of her yet. So we sat in the bus, watching through steamy windows the growing crowd of children braving the rain to come and investigate us. Phil and Jay prepared their filming equipment, pulling out yet again the waterproof covering for the cameras so they could film in the rain.

Eventually we spotted Jeannette, picking her way carefully up the path, a huge black umbrella shielding her from the worst of the rain. It had begun to ease off a little now, but she must have left her house as the tropical downpour was at its worst, presumably with her concern to respect the arranged time outweighing her distaste for getting soaked! The path to her house was down a fairly steep slope, riveted with gullies where the torrential rain had repeatedly swept away tons of red-brown, sticky mud. We stepped gingerly over drenched, muddy grass and little rushing streams, anxious not to slide and fall over on the treacherously slippery path.

It was Sunday, and we hadn't had time to change after church in the morning, so with one hand holding my umbrella, the other was gathering up my ankle-length skirt. Fortunately it was reddish-brown in colour anyway. But at least we had flat shoes on, unlike Jeannette's high-heeled, strappy sandals!

Leaving our umbrellas and mud-caked shoes on the covered front porch, we all piled into Jeannette's sitting room. We had realised earlier that the presence of all six of us might a bit too intimidating for Jeannette, so Sue, Jay, Ray and Bosco were to go back quite soon to the bus, leaving me to talk alone with Jeannette – with only Phil and his camera.

But there was a slight problem. As we sat chatting for a few minutes in the sitting room, to my dismay a visitor walked in, attracted no doubt by the strange sight of a group of *bazungu* in the neighbourhood. Although introduced to this man, I had no idea if he was a close friend or just an inquisitive onlooker. And without knowing whether or not he was trustworthy, it would be impossible to talk openly with Jeannette. I motioned to Jeannette to step outside with me for a moment where I could ask her and, as I'd suspected, she too was unhappy to talk in his presence.

Knowing it would be completely inappropriate to ask this man to leave, I asked if there was somewhere else we could sit and chat in private.

'Yes, there's the guest room,' she replied immediately, obviously equally keen to have privacy. 'We could sit in there.'

In years past I would have found it odd, if not rude, to leave a guest sitting alone while I disappeared through the back of the house. But I had been on the receiving end of such behaviour so many times that I'd even begun to practise it myself – particularly if the visitor was hardly known to me, seemed to have come simply out of curiosity and was showing no signs of leaving! Jeannette appeared quite unperturbed about leaving this particular visitor.

The guest room was dark, with grey concrete walls and floor and only one tiny window. But pulling back the little curtain revealed two beds, one of which was piled with an assortment of clothing and blankets. The door to this room led off the sitting room, and as neither door nor ceilings were very well fitting, clearly voices would carry easily. Fortunately, however, the rain battering on the corrugated tin roof made it almost impossible even to hear each other, even though we were close, so there was no way that the visitor in the sitting room could have heard us.

Phil sat on one bed, his back to the window. Jeannette and I sat opposite, allowing the little light there was to shine directly onto us. Jeannette spoke softly, relating to me the events of the middle of April 1994. The facts she gave were much the same as I had heard from Apollonie but there were a few extra details. Charles had apparently arrived at the diocese wearing several layers of clothing. He had been very shaken by events in Rwamagana before he left. Apparently the militia had begun to beat him up before he was recognised by a senior army man who ordered them away. He had come to Butare – smuggled here in the back of the car of his military friend who was evacuating his family to Congo – because he thought it would be safe, as it had been in 1990⁻ when the war had not reached so far south.

There was nothing particularly surprising in the details Jeannette gave, but it was agonising to imagine how Charles must have been feeling at the time. The terror of being attacked, having to flee across country, knowing that at any moment he might be stopped and killed.

She spoke of his few days at the diocese in Butare and of the day the military had arrived to take him away. Although reluctant to be specific, it was clear from her comments about Pastor Kabalira that she felt he had had a significant part to play in betraying both Charles and her husband. She spoke of how frequently and uncharacteristically Kabalira had visited their house in these early days of the genocide. Like so many others, she was convinced he was collaborating with the militia.

In May, soon after giving birth to her firstborn – a terrifying experience in the midst of the killings – the militia burst into Jeannette and Philip's house. Jeannette herself was in a back bedroom, feeding her daughter, but her husband and his sister were in the sitting room. Presumably taking the sister to be Jeannette, the militia took both Philip and his sister, leaving Jeannette unnoticed but utterly terrified in the bedroom. From then until the end of the genocide in early July, she did not dare to leave the house.

Listening to Jeannette I was impressed by how she seemed to have coped with such awful experiences. She displayed neither the bitterness and anger nor the emotional detachment I had so often seen. There was still a raw sadness in what she shared, but somehow it was tempered with a glimmer of hope and optimism in a gentle, gracious manner. She could face the past honestly but was also moving on now in her life with her ten-year-old daughter. There was a genuineness about her that I felt I could almost trust.

She talked for some time about the events of April and May 1994 but there was more I wanted to know. Eventually I plucked up courage to ask her the question that had haunted me now for years.

'In these few days that you spent together, did Charles mention me at all? I mean, did he say anything about what had happened between us, or how he felt about it all?' Jeannette shook her head.

'He didn't talk of you at all,' she replied. 'Not to me anyway. There was too much else going on. I wanted to ask him how things were between you, but I was waiting for the right moment, you know. And then it was too late.'

But she *had* known about our problems. So the news had travelled as far as Butare then. I asked how she had heard about it.

'You maybe don't remember me,' she said, 'but I used to live in Gahini before I was married. I worked for Compassion. That's how I knew Charles and why he came to see us when he came to Butare. I'm godmother to his nephew who used to live with you.' I'm afraid I didn't remember her. There were a lot of people in Gahini I had probably met but didn't know. Rwandans were much better than me at remembering names and details – and I guess they had the advantage of there being only a handful of us expatriates to recognise.

'I lived down the hill, beside Canon Kajuga,' she continued. 'I shared a house with Martine, you know.' My heart missed a beat. Jeannette had shared a house with Martine, the secretary at the school where Charles had worked! So she would have seen Charles coming to visit at night. She would be able to confirm or refute the rumours that had started spreading about him half way through our marriage. This was completely unexpected.

'So was it true,' I asked, 'that Charles had started having an affair with Martine only a few months after we were married?' Not only a few months later, Jeannette confirmed, but before, during and right the way through our marriage. Both she and her neighbour Canon Kajuga had tried on several occasions to talk sense into him, telling him it was totally inappropriate to be spending so much time with Martine while his wife was waiting for him at home, but he didn't see it as a problem.

I tried to take in this information but my mind was in a blur. I had been expecting to hear from Jeannette about Charles' last days in Butare, not to hear of his affair with Martine, having tried for years to disbelieve it and give him the benefit of the doubt. I had had no idea that the woman who, with her husband, had given Charles meals and kindness in the days before he died would be the same one who had witnessed his repeated betrayal of me, his wife.

'But why did no one tell me about it,' I asked, still struggling to grasp what she was saying. 'I must have looked really stupid, if everyone else knew expect for me.' 'I guess we were hoping his friendship would fizzle out when you got married,' she replied. 'Quite often a man will have friendships with a few women when he's single, but he leaves them behind when he gets married. But then, when he didn't, I suppose people thought you wouldn't believe them anyway.'

I thought back to the two women who had come to inform me of Charles' affair. How bitterly I resented them at the time for spreading such malicious and destructive gossip. But were they actually the brave ones who did try to tell me and, as Jeannette said, I didn't want to hear?

'When Charles left you and moved to Rwamagana, Martine had also moved away from Gahini,' she continued. 'I believe they were planning to move to Gitarama together.' That was another rumour that had reached my ears all those years ago but that I'd chosen to ignore, because I couldn't bear the possibility that it might be true.

For the rest of our time with Jeannette my mind was in a haze. I was listening to what she said, but not taking it in. Somehow I had to pass on the barest minimum of information to Phil who was patiently and discreetly filming the whole conversation.

'I'm hearing some unpalatable details of the extent of Charles' relationship with Martine,' I managed to say. 'I'll tell you about it later.' At that moment I was glad to have Phil there. Even though he could not understand one word of our conversation I knew he would be sympathetic. I had shared a lot with the team about the difficulties in our marriage and really appreciated their understanding and support.

In the days after that meeting with Jeannette I did wonder whether or not she was telling the truth. People invent all sorts of stories, to discredit those they don't like, and then spread them around as if true. That's why it's almost impossible to determine the truth surrounding the crimes committed during the genocide. Over the years twisted versions of events have become 'truth' to those who invented them. Maybe if Jeannette had had a grudge against Martine for some reason she could have sought to damage her reputation in this way.

But Jeannette's clear and straightforward account of events and her gracious, gentle attitude did not in any way lead me to think of her as a compulsive liar. And much of what she said I had also heard from her former neighbours, the Kajugas, whom I knew well and for whom I had great respect. So I had to believe it was true.

Jeannette accompanied us back up the slippery muddy slope to the bus, and we said goodbye, promising to keep in touch. If, or rather when, the Butare *Gacaca* court eventually got off the ground, Jeannette's evidence concerning the circumstances around the deaths of both Charles and Philip would surely be key. I hoped she would have the courage to go and speak out.

I felt as though this meeting had been hugely significant for me but I would need time to process it. As we travelled on in the bus towards Kigali I related the news to Sue. Talking it through helped me to grasp the implications of what I'd just heard. For so long I'd hung onto the hope that the rumours were false, that one day we might have got back together again. But now that had all gone. I had to face the truth. Our marriage had failed. Charles had been unfaithful to me.

I think what hurt me most was the realisation that I had been lied to throughout the whole time we were together. I had struggled so much with his frequent absences in the evenings, and the vagueness of his explanations, but for so long I blamed myself for being suspicious and not trusting him. Now I was beginning to see that it all added up. But it would take time to sink in.

Sue commented on how hard she found it to equate the Charles I had just been hearing about with the Charles she had known, albeit briefly. And she was right. He was a lovely guy. He had won the hearts of all my family and friends when we visited the UK in the summer of 1993. They loved his easygoing, friendly nature. That's what made it all the harder to see this other side of him. I could only assume that he did not intentionally mean to hurt me.

But hurt me he did. Profoundly. And after the cool-headed accounting of the facts, the tears flowed. As the bus sped on its way to Kigali, the compassionate silence in the bus was punctuated only by my muffled sobs on Sue's shoulder as she hugged me tightly. Now I just wanted to go home. I was weary, confused and I'd had enough. What was the point of continuing a search for the killers of the man who had himself so painfully betrayed me? I felt so angry towards him. Hope had gone. The hope of what might have been had things worked out between us. The hope of getting to the bottom of the mystery of his disappearance. Gone was my motivation for seeing justice done and seeking to forgive.

How could I ever contemplate forgiving his murderers when I could not forgive him?

But I couldn't go home. We had been in Rwanda for less than a week and I was not my own boss. I had a schedule to follow. I knew there would be worse to come, but I also knew that to give up at this stage would be of no benefit to anyone in the long run – least of all me. With the support of the crew and the contacts they had made there was a strong possibility of finding out exactly what had happened. Yes, I had been betrayed, and yes, I had been hurt. But life had carried on and would still carry on.

In fact, the more I thought about it, strange as it may seem, the more I began to realise how releasing it was to have discovered the truth. After years of uncertainty, and even though the news was terrible to hear, yet somehow knowing the truth gave me a sense of freedom. I had nothing to fear from gossiping behind my back. I could embrace failure as a normal part of life and hold my head up without shame. It's true, there would still be some painful revisiting of familiar places and seeing them again through different eyes, but perhaps even that would be a positive part of healing and moving on.

5

Liliose

Our taxi driver and his mate were very patient men. Loading, unloading and lugging around the piles of luggage and heavy equipment that came with us everywhere was never too much trouble for them. They had to put up with changed plans, unexpected journeys and *lots* of hanging around. But then taxi drivers in Rwanda were used to that. Life is never quite predictable here.

Today's journey, however, was going to be their biggest challenge yet – and maybe ours too. We didn't have an address for Liliose – at least, not an address as we in the UK would understand it. But as I had suspected, the crew had discovered some crucial information on their previous trip. They had been able to make contact with Liliose's relative Paulette at her work place and had been given a small scrap of paper with a few words written on it. It said GITARAMA – Mucyakabiri – Nyabikenke – Centre Remera – Aunt Asterie (Btique). Well... we could always ask along the way, couldn't we? It surely wouldn't be that difficult to find. The plan was to set off fairly early in the morning to allow plenty of time for the travelling and quality time with Liliose.

Early morning overlooking Kigali is stunning. The room Sue and I were in must have been the best one in our small hotel. We had a massive balcony – big enough for twenty people to sit around – and with a fabulous view right over the city. It had rained heavily in the night and the mist was still hanging low in pockets between the hills, but already the city was alive. Voices called back and forth. The streets were filling with people – people walking to work, walking to market, walking to school, and nimbly leaping into the grass verges to avoid the splashes from passing cars bumping along the puddle-strewn road. I loved this time of day.

While I stood pondering on the balcony, Sue had popped into the bathroom. But she emerged again immediately. 'There's no water,' she announced, 'not even any cold.' Hmm. Lovely hotel, beautiful location – but no water. Oh well, we can't have everything! But I figured they must have a tank somewhere for times like this so I went off on the scrounge. Just half a bucketful each would be more than enough to make ourselves presentable before being cooped up in a stuffy minibus with eight people all day.

At the bottom of the stairs there was a large room open on one side to the outside courtyard. It looked as if this was where all the activity took place. Soggy hotel towels hung on a couple of lines in the inside part. How does anything dry in this wet weather? There were two large sinks in one corner, an ironing board and baskets in another, and piles of large tins and boxes strewn over tables everywhere else. In the courtyard outside a man and a woman were busy over a couple of charcoal stoves. Breakfast?

'Good morning,' I called through. 'You're busy!' They returned my greeting, looking a bit amused to see a *muzungu* wandering into their kitchen, but quite unperturbed. 'Sorry to bother you, but we've got no water. Any chance of taking a bucketful up with me?' It was the electricity cuts, the woman explained. They were happening quite frequently these days. But not to worry, her colleague would bring me some up straight away. 'Oh, er, don't worry,' I said, unwilling to go without the water in case we might have to wait ages for it to arrive. 'I can manage it – it's not heavy.'

Half an hour later the inconvenience of the lack of water

was more than compensated for by the fantastic breakfast brought out to us. A hot fresh omelette each, a large pile of bread with lashings of gooseberry jam and a plate of fresh fruit each – pineapple, papaya, tree tomatoes and bananas. What's more, my friend Elsie, Nicholas' wife, turned up half way through with a massive thermos for me full of *sosoma*, my favourite porridge. We wouldn't be hungry for a while.

We left a bit later than intended, so Apollonie was already waiting by the side of the road when we drew up. It was good that she was coming with us to Butare. I knew I'd be very glad of her company the following day at the com-memorations of the tenth anniversary of the genocide. She'd have to put up with our day searching out Liliose, but she could cope with that, especially having met Liliose's mum, Anatolie, at our wedding.

I was terribly excited at the prospect of seeing Liliose again. We all were! The last time I had seen her was in the refugee camps in Tanzania in 1995. She had been staying in a different camp from most of my Gahini friends, and I had no transport to get over there to see her. But someone had sent word that I wanted to see her, so she was brought over by the woman with whom she was living. After that I lost contact with her.

The camps were emptied in 1996, so I presumed she had gone back to Rwanda, but my attempts to track her down had always failed. At that time, still very soon after the genocide, and with such insecurity over the country, perhaps people were afraid of asking too many questions or giving any information. You never knew what rumours might be spread about you. Maybe it was too risky. Best to keep your head down.

But I had always worried about her well-being. I didn't know if she had any surviving family or whether she was being well cared for. Her mother had been devoted to her daughters. They were much loved and had had a secure and happy first few years of their lives. It was awful to think of this little girl suddenly being completely bereft of her entire family and all that had made up her young life.

I knew she would have no tangible reminders of her family – no photographs or mementos. The woman who rescued her and fled with her to Tanzania must have left in a great rush, probably not even having time to take any of her own possessions. I too had left all my photos behind, but a few people in the UK who'd visited me in Rwanda had their own photos and sent me copies. So I'd been able to put together a small album of photos of Anatolie, Liliose and her late sister Mireille. At least it would be a little reminder she could keep of the family she'd once had.

The scrap of paper said she lived in Gitarama. I knew the town of Gitarama a little bit. We would pass through it on the road to Butare and it wasn't very big, so it shouldn't be too hard to find Liliose's aunt, I thought. But I'd forgotten that Gitarama was also the name of this particular prefecture or region of Rwanda, and as such is a much larger area than just the town.

Just on the outskirts of the town we found the area known as Mucyakabiri and on a muddy road heading off to the right there was a signpost pointing to Nyabikenke. Great! The first three names on our list. We're well on the way now, I thought, as we turned onto the bumpy road and headed off in the direction of Nyabikenke. Now let's look out for any sign of Remera. Shouldn't be too far.

Two-and-a-half hours later we were still bumping along. We had, of course, stopped to ask several people on the way. Some promised us it was not too far – 'just half an hour,' said one. Then twenty minutes later, 'it'll be at least an hour, maybe 25 kilometres," said another. But how do you measure time or distance for a vehicle when you only travel by foot or bicycle? One elderly gentleman brought his hand over his mouth. 'Remera? Eh, eh, eh, eh, eh. *Ni kure*,' he said, in that disconcerting Rwandan way of expressing shock. 'It's a *very* long way.'

We decided to reassess the situation. Already it was early afternoon. The rain had held off so far, fortunately – probably the first day since we'd arrived when it hadn't rained! But the sky was looking ominous. It would be dark by 6.30 p.m. and I knew the driver would not be happy to drive this road in the dark and certainly not if it rained.

Apart from the steep drops down the mountain beside the road, hairpin bends and massive pot-holes, we had crossed a number of little bridges over streams – well, to call them bridges was maybe a bit of an exaggeration. They consisted of only a few solid logs, carefully positioned to the width of minibus wheels. The driver's mate would jump out to watch the alignment of the wheels on the passenger side, while the driver inched along carefully, hanging out of his window checking the wheels on his own side, front and back. Bad enough when the logs were dry, but try negotiating that in the dark with wet, slippery logs and a tiny trickle that had turned into a raging torrent underneath us! Maybe not the best way to keep on good terms with our driver. Reason said we should turn back. But there was such a sense of anticipation in that minibus and we'd all be terribly disappointed to give up now. I asked the driver what he'd rather do. 'Let's carry on,' he said, without a moment's hesitation, 'as long as you don't spend too long there and we get back before dark.' Yes!

Not much further on we rounded a corner and came across a very smart, pale-brick building with bright blue corrugated tin roof and high metal fence around it. *Banki y'Abaturage*, it announced on a smart, brightly coloured board behind the fence. A bank! Having driven for hours through very rural countryside where the few houses around were made mostly of mud, this seemed so out of place. But suddenly there were lots more buildings around – a small village centre. We had arrived in Remera.

The setting reminded me a little of a Wild West movie, only without the horses. A long low row of roughly built mud and cement buildings lined the wide, packed-earth main street on both sides. A few people sat around in front of open doors, shaded under awnings from the heat of the afternoon sun, sipping beer from a gourd. Ours was almost the only vehicle, so our arrival caused a bit of a stir – in a half-interested, siesta-time kind of way.

I knew from my piece of paper that Liliose's Aunt Asterie had a shop here, so I wandered over to an open door with a sign 'Boutique' above it. A woman stood outside. Might this be Asterie, I wondered, as I approached her. Did she look like Liliose? We must be so close to finding her now. I could feel my excitement growing.

No, this was not Asterie, but she lived close by, we were told. A woman had been standing nearby watching us and agreed to lead us to her house. We followed her along a track, climbing up behind the main street. I found myself wondering what it might be like to live in this place. We were nearly 3 hours' drive away from the main road. It felt like the middle of nowhere! Yet there were a few well-built, attractive houses along this path. Whitewashed walls, substantial fences festooned with bright pink and orange bougainvillea, front yards swept spotlessly clean. As we walked on I felt a strange malaise deep inside me. Why? I wasn't going to be living here, so what was bothering me? The fact was, had Charles and I still been living in Rwanda we might have lived in a house like one of these, in a village like this. I remembered how I used to feel when recently married, how I desperately wanted to belong, to feel at home. But somehow I always felt like an outsider, lonely, misunderstood, a failure. I had tried so hard to change, to fit in, but now I realise that by doing so I had been losing the real me. Had we carried on living in Rwanda, perhaps moving to a place like this, what would have happened to *me*? What if I were to come back and live in Rwanda now? Could I yet belong here? Of course I was not really conscious of these thoughts at the time. All I knew was that the white houses, the bougainvillea, and the shy, smiling children around had momentarily stirred something deep within me. Only months later, as I search to understand, am I beginning to be honest with myself and acknowledge some of these feelings.

At that moment there was no time to stop and reflect, for we were following the woman through the gate of one of these houses, and might be about to see Liliose. It had been nine years since I'd last seen her. I'd pretty much given up hope of ever being able to track her down or see her again. But the film crew's enthusiastic researching had led us to this place – and at last I was going to meet her again!

Rather than knocking at the front door like a guest, our guide headed round the side of the house to the back yard. I followed her quickly, my heart racing. A teenage girl was bent over a large plastic tub full of soap suds and clothes. As we appeared she straightened up, wiped her hands down the sides of the *kanga* cloth with which she was wrapped, and shyly extended a limp wrist for us to shake in greeting. In these few seconds I was scrutinising her face. Could this be Liliose? Were there any similarities to the Liliose I remembered from nine years previously? Was there any hint of recognition in her eyes as she looked at me?

But no. We were not there yet. This was a girl who helped with the housework, not Liliose. 'You've just missed her,' she told us, looking somewhat bemused by this strange bunch of *bazungu* in her back yard. 'She's gone to hospital. But she's not ill,' she added, seeing the immediate concern on my face. 'She's just taking some food to a sick friend. She won't be long. You could go and meet her on the way if you like. The hospital's just over there,' she said, pointing in the direction of a hilltop across the valley. There was clearly a footpath leading down through the valley and up the side of the opposite hill, but what wasn't clear to me was how many hills beyond that we'd have to walk over to reach the hospital. 'Just over there' could mean anything. So we decided to go back to the vehicle and drive there on the road.

Before leaving, however, there was some conversation about where Aunt Asterie would be and whether we should go to find her first. She had apparently gone off in the opposite direction to a 'burial of the bones' ceremony.[3] But our time was limited and I didn't want to lose precious minutes, so I asked the driver to take us straight to the hospital. However, somewhere along the line, in a discussion between the driver, his mate, our translator and maybe even the little boy sent to direct us, my request must have been overruled. Because ten minutes later, with no hospital anywhere in sight, we drew up at the side of the road opposite a huge crowd. Heads turned to stare at us and several angry young men started a heated exchange with our driver. For some reason unknown to me the driver had taken us to the 'burial of the bones' ceremony instead. Was Liliose here perhaps, rather than at the hospital? Or had it been decided that we should find Aunt Asterie before looking for Liliose? Maybe I had misunderstood the information given to us. It wouldn't be the first time!

A couple of armed policemen had come to join the growing group around our minibus and they clearly weren't happy to see the cameras sitting on Jay's and Phil's laps. I wasn't following much of the arguing going on around us, but since we had no desire to disrupt the funeral ceremonies surely we could at least move the vehicle a couple of hundred yards along the road away from the crowds. This did seem to pacify them a bit and we were then able to get out of the bus.

As we stood around, and as conversations continued, I still had no idea what was going on, but I saw two ladies leave the crowd and head purposefully towards us. One of them, I was told, was Aunt Asterie! To this day I still don't know how they knew we were looking for them or how they were found so quickly in that vast crowd of people. But then how lots of things 'just happen' in Rwanda remains a mystery to me!

Greetings all around, brief introductions and exchange of

news, a quick check to ascertain that Liliose was not actually with her but had indeed gone to the hospital, and it was back into the minibus – together with Aunt Asterie and her friend. Now our numbers had swelled to twelve. But even with all our luggage piled in the back we were still luxuriously comfortable compared to the quantities of people, animals, bags and mattresses usually crammed into a Rwandan minibus taxi.

We set off again – this time, finally, to the hospital where we would find Liliose. Perhaps our driver and translator had thought it wise to make contact with Asterie first and not go straight to Liliose. I was glad to be guided by them in matters of discretion and local protocol – it just would be nice to know what was actually going on sometimes and not feel left in the dark!

It had always been a dilemma for me to get a balance between pushing my own agenda on the one hand and backing off out of respect for cultural norms and expectations on the other. Liliose's mum, Anatolie, had been an expert in this. She was discreet and respectful in her dealings with our health workers – but she could certainly speak her mind and challenge when necessary. No one could pull the wool over her eyes! But she was no longer here. Again I felt angry at the senseless waste of her life. Why, oh why, was she murdered? I wondered how much Liliose would remember now of what happened that day, or even what she might remember of her mother. When I had talked to her ten years ago she had been only four years old and extremely traumatised. Might she remember more now? And I wondered too about how I would react to seeing her again. I was excited, yes, but also beginning to feel daunted by the prospect of facing grief again and sharing it with someone so young whose life had been so devastated. The baseline of both our stories was tragic – as with so many people here. And so any joy in reunion always had a constant shadow of grief skulking in the background.

The minibus bumped and lurched its way back down the side of one hill and up another, winding round hairpin bends, meandering through trees and between patchworks of small, cultivated fields. This central region of Rwanda was almost new to me, and different from the eastern side where I'd lived. The hills were steeper here, and more densely packed. There was more woodland and fewer banana plantations. Different, but equally stunningly beautiful.

Another fifteen or twenty minutes' driving, and eventually we pulled up outside a series of long, low brick buildings on the top of a hill. Funny, Gahini hospital was built on the top of a hill too. Fantastic views, of course, but it makes for an exhausting steep climb to reach it when you're sick – and a long way to have to collect water daily from the valley below.

Once again we all piled out of the minibus while someone slipped off to look for Liliose. The next few minutes seemed like an eternity. We had come all this way to find Liliose, and any moment now she would appear out from one of these buildings. We had tracked her down at last – or had we? For the news came back that she'd already left and would be on her way back home. Oh, no! If she'd gone off down the footpath she would be quite some time in getting home (it seemed the distance was quite a bit further than the worker had implied!) and it was getting too late to wait any longer. But there was one last chance. Bosco, our ever-enthusiastic and youthful translator was dispatched off down the path at the run to see if he could catch up with her and bring her back. Sue and I set off slowly in the same direction he had gone. Though it was late afternoon the sun was still beating down strongly and there was no shade on the path. We wandered along slowly, our eyes scanning the distant path where it disappeared round the side of the hill.

At last, around the corner in the far distance, we saw two small figures approaching. As they drew nearer we recognised the colour of Bosco's T-shirt, and the other... the other must surely be Liliose. I speeded up my pace walking towards them.

'Liliose?' I asked tentatively as she approached. The girl's eyes were focussed on the ground, her face barely visible. As I spoke she lifted her head and her eyes met mine briefly before returning to the earth below.

'*Karame,*' she mumbled in reply – the polite response given when summoned by name. So it really was her! Yes, I recognised her. She had changed, of course, over the years, but there in front of me was the face of the little four-year-old girl who used to come to my house hand in hand with her protective big sister, bringing me lettuces from their garden. Here at last was Liliose.

How I longed just to throw my arms around her and hold onto each other, as I had done with Gemima and John, with young Suzanne, and with so many others. But she evidently didn't recognise me and was, understandably, keeping a clear physical and emotional distance.

'I'm Lesley Bilinda,' I explained to her. 'I used to live in Gahini and worked with your mum. She was a good friend of mine, when you were a little girl. Do you remember me?' She looked up to my face searchingly.

'No,' she half whispered, shaking her head slightly.

'I came to visit you when you were living in Tanzania, in the refugee camps.' I tried again. 'You were brought over from your camp to see me. Do you remember that time?' This time there was a glimmer of recognition. She lifted her head and eyebrows simultaneously, uttering a soft 'eeyh' sound. This was definitely an affirmative. I took her hand and tried to chat as we walked slowly back towards the bus. But her responses were barely audible and monosyllabic. She seemed completely overwhelmed by this reception committee sent out to meet her. Was it the thought of five *bazungu* searching for her? Was it the cameras focussed on us from every angle? Was it seeing me again, and my association with her mother and her life in Gahini? There was so much I wanted to ask her and tell her, but all the very personal conversation would have to wait till we were back at her house and in the privacy of a room alone together. So, as we walked then drove off in the minibus, I tried to keep conversation to a general level. I discovered she was in her first year at secondary school, that English was her favourite subject, and that there was a post-office box number for the school so I would be able to write to her. But most of the time she was staring out of the window or down at her hands on her lap, and again kept her responses to a minimum.

Was she just terribly shy? Or still traumatised after her dreadful experiences back in 1994? Or was she perhaps very unhappy at home? Her father's sister had taken her in, and clearly she was able to attend school and was adequately clothed and fed. But was she loved? So many families in Rwanda had taken in the orphaned children of their relatives, often at great sacrifice because of the extra demands placed on already very limited budgets. But I was often saddened to see – even in educated Christian families – that the adopted children were treated as second-class citizens and kept on the periphery of family life. They would be provided for materially with the essentials for life – food, shelter, clothing and often education – but there would be little affection, love or sense of being wanted and belonging.

I knew nothing yet about Liliose's home situation, but I knew this could be a possibility. I would probably never find out, of course, because she would not dare to tell me, and her aunt would no doubt be charming as long as visitors were around. I could only observe and reflect.

Back in Remera, we left the minibus in the village centre again and headed back up the hill towards Aunt Asterie's house. But not before our driver had called me aside.

'Erm, it's getting a bit late you know. You won't be too long, will you? We'll need to go soon.' I assured him we wouldn't delay. We had made contact. I had an address for keeping in touch with Liliose. And I only had a couple of things to chat to her about. We would only be a few minutes, I promised.

Once in the sitting room it would have been polite for us all to sit and chat together for a while before getting down to the business of why we had come. But there was no time for this leisurely custom. I took Liliose aside and asked if we could sit somewhere privately, in her room perhaps. She took me behind a curtain into a room off the sitting room and we sat together on the bed. Of course nowhere is exactly private when Phil and his camera are only six feet away, but the main thing was that Liliose was out of earshot of her family.

I took out the little photo album I had prepared for her. 'These are some photos of you and your mum and your sister,' I explained softly. 'They are for you to keep to help you remember the lovely family you had.' We turned over the pages of the album. 'Look, here's your mum at work chatting to one of the clients. And here she is in Congo when we were on a course there together. Do you remember her at all?' Liliose stared intently at the photographs, and shook her head.

'She was a lovely mum, Liliose. She loved you a lot.' I wanted her to know that even if the worst scenario was true and there was little love around for her as an adopted member of this family, she had once been a wanted and much-treasured child with a good, caring mother. 'You and your sister Mireille were very special to her. Look, here's you and Mireille when you were about three years old.' She looked closely at the photos but her face remained expressionless. I asked her how old she was now, maybe about fourteen?

'No,' she told me. 'I'm twelve. I was born in 1992.' I thought for a moment. 'Actually, Liliose, I think you must be fourteen, because you were born in 1990.'

'No,' she said again, emphatically. 'That was my sister. The one who died. That's what they told me.'

This was a strange conversation to be having and I began

to question my own memory. But then, she was now with her father's side of the family who had lived a long way from Gahini, and perhaps they had not been in close contact before 1994. So maybe they themselves were not too sure of Liliose's background.

We turned over to a picture of her mother very heavily pregnant in a pink spotted dress. 'This was in 1990,' I explained, 'only a few months after I arrived in Rwanda. Your mum was pregnant with twins, and one of them was you. I remember when you were born. Your twin was not so strong as you and sadly she died. So you were definitely born in 1990, Liliose. You had another sister, Mireille – the one in the photos. She was a couple of years older than you, but she died from malaria in February 1994. It was a very sad time.'

She gave no response whatsoever and I have no idea if she believed what I told her. Why should she, when it contradicted what she had known for ten years? What would it be like to learn of a sister you never knew you had, and to discover that you're two years older than you'd always believed? I could only leave it with her, and maybe talk further through letters if she wanted.

We finished looking through the album and I placed it in her hands. 'There will be times when it makes you very sad to look at this, and to remember your lovely family. I expect sometimes you'll cry a lot. But I want you always to remember how much you were loved by them. And I want you to know that I love you too,' I added. 'I've come all this way looking for you because you and your family are special to me. I hope we can keep in contact, Liliose. I'll write to you at school.'

Our time was running out, so I suggested I pray with her before I left. Anatolie had had a real faith and wanted her children to share it. When Mireille had died Anatolie had responded with great courage and trust in God, and not a hint of bitterness. I knew she would want Liliose to hold onto God, even if all else around her felt bleak.

We emerged from the bedroom to join the others waiting in the sitting room, said our thanks to Aunt Asterie for her hospitality – she presented us with a stick of bananas to take with us in the bus – and started back down the hill towards the bus. All the family and neighbouring kids joined us on the walk back, including a girl a few years older who lives with her – Liliose's cousin. To my enormous relief I noticed the two girls nudging each other, whispering and giggling together. So there was at least one person here with whom Liliose was at ease, and she was obviously not without a bit of fun in her life.

It was hard to leave Liliose. I felt we had breezed in and out of her life, probably leaving her spinning from what she had seen and heard. And even if she wasn't, I certainly was. I was feeling quite overwhelmed at finding her at last after all these years. But it was also worrying to see her very flat response and frustrating that I wouldn't have any more opportunities to spend time with her and really find out how she was.

A couple of weeks later, when back in the UK, I began to worry that my visit might actually have been quite disturbing for her. Maybe she had learned to survive by blocking her traumatic experiences out of her mind completely. Would looking at the pictures reawaken the horrors of the past? And what would she do with the memories and feelings if it did? Post-traumatic stress debriefing or trauma counselling would no doubt be impossible to come by in the remote areas of her home and her school.

I shared my concerns with a clinical psychologist friend highly experienced in working with victims of trauma. She reassured me that the psyche often has a way of holding such awful experiences until the person is in a context that feels safe enough to begin to face and deal with them. Perhaps it would be many years yet before Liliose could let these memories surface. In the meantime, just learning of a family that had loved her, and of friends who had come half way around the world to see her again, might begin to fit in some of the missing pieces in a positive way. Certainly I could hope that this would be the case.

It was nearly dark by the time we bumped off the rough road from Remera back, with relief, onto the tarmac road in Gitarama. And it was dark and late by the time we eventually reached Butare. When the crew had spent time in Butare earlier in the year the Bishop of Butare had been extremely helpful, insisting that when we all came back in April Sue and I should stay in his own guest rooms. However, despite the convenience of mobile phones we'd been unable to contact him to tell him we were coming. So we decided to try a small hotel on the edge of town. The crew had stayed there before and knew it was fine.

But there was no room. It was 6 April. The next day there would be major commemorations happening in the town for the tenth anniversary of the beginning of the genocide. The town would be full of visitors, wise enough to arrive before dark! Perhaps we'd need to try the Bishop after all, despite the late hour. To his credit and our relief he immediately arranged for us to stay – Sue and myself in his own little guest rooms, and the others in the diocesan guest-house.

It was hard to be back in Butare again – and especially staying at the diocese, the very place where Charles had spent his last days alive. These next days were going to be crucial in our journey to track down his killers. This was the place where I hoped to get the information I needed and maybe even meet them, if they were still in the country. It was going to be a very tough time – and it would start straight away the next morning when we joined in the commemorations of the deaths of the tens of thousands who were murdered in this town ten years ago.

6

Memorial March

I began the morning of Wednesday 7 April feeling heavy in my heart. I was tired from the travelling of the previous day, had not slept well, and was weighed down with the anticipation of the day ahead. Although the President of Rwanda had been killed in the evening of 6 April 1994, the genocide did not begin in earnest until the seventh – hence this date has been chosen as a day of national mourning throughout the country. The atmosphere was extremely heavy leading up to this day.

We were planning to join the commemoration march beginning at the main genocide memorial site, walking through the centre of town and congregating at the town's football stadium. It seemed straightforward enough, but for some reason there was debate as to which memorial site was to be the starting point. Which was the one I had been to before? I was asked. Could I describe where it was or what it looked like?

Having only been to Butare briefly in 1995, and at that time paying very little attention to the surroundings, I had no idea where we were supposed to be, was not aware of other memorial sites, and was beginning to get irritated by the indecision and questions. All I knew was that I wanted to be at the memorial site where I had been in 1995 and where I thought Charles might be buried.

Then there was the question of scarves. To show solidarity all the marchers were to be wearing purple scarves, the Bishop told us over breakfast. This was news to us, and of course by that time it was too late to find anywhere to buy them. The idea did cross my mind that a bishop's clerical purple shirt would be about the right colour and would divide nicely between six people, but I thought better than to suggest it.

I could not know for certain where Charles had been buried. It was only a possibility that it had been at the site of the current memorial. But I believed he had been taken around the twentieth or twenty-first of April 1994, when the moderate mayor of Butare had been replaced by a hardliner and the killings had suddenly spread. Back in 1995 I had been told that the people killed around that time had been thrown into a particular mass grave that had just been excavated. And so it was to a ceremony for the reburial of the bones of these people that I had come in October 1995, having been told about it in a letter from my sister-in-law, Apollonie.

I remember the circumstances well. We gathered at the university stadium, the site where so many thousands had been slaughtered. There were rows of politicians, dignitaries and church leaders as well as hundreds of ordinary citizens and it was all highly official and formal. After the speeches, prayers and celebration of Mass, we formed a huge snake procession, walking slowly down a twisting road through trees to the prepared site below. We followed an open-topped lorry piled high with coffins.

It was rainy season then too, and the burial site was awash with mud. Huge pits had been dug into the ground, each one being gradually filled with coffin after coffin. Rows upon rows of coffins, each containing the bones of many people. It was a desperate sight. How many thousands of people were being reburied here? And yet this only represented those killed in one location at one particular time. This scene could be repeated hundreds of times over, all around the country, so vast was the extent of the killings during those dreadful three months.

As well as the fresh graves, there was a small covered but open-sided tent with only a large table inside. On the table were laid out dozens of skulls. I could not bear to look and stood most of the time with my back to this table.

There was a lot of standing around on that day. The rain had hampered the preparation of the site, so digging was still taking place. Instructions and information were blasted through an amplifier system, large loudspeakers strung from tree to tree. During the long wait we were subjected to loud music through this system. The waiting around had allowed the heavy atmosphere to lift a little, so when the song 'Tie a Yellow Ribbon Round the Old Oak Tree' came booming through the trees, I couldn't help but laugh at the surrealism of the situation.

That was nine years previously. I had not been back to Butare since then. So when it was eventually decided where the memorial site was, and we arrived there, it was little wonder I did not recognise it at all. The area had mostly been concreted over and surrounded by crazy paving. At one end a kind of concrete gazebo housing a memorial plaque was still being painted in the memorial purple colour. Between this building and the roadside a handful of men were mixing and laying concrete between bricks that edged a large solid triangular post with the words 'UNR Genocide Memorial' in Kinyarwandan, English and French, one language on each side.

As I looked around I realised we were a little downhill from the university, surrounded by trees – so this could well have been the place to which we had come in 1995. But it had certainly changed.

A crowd gathered around to hear the speeches and prayers, little of which I understood. I stood quietly, weighed down with the enormity of the occasion, images of genocide –

both remembered and imagined – filling my mind. In time the crowd began to move off, gathering numbers as we walked slowly through the town centre. Many carried banners bearing Kinyarwandan, English or French slogans such as 'Where were the UN and the International Community?' or 'You have been gone for ten years. We will never forget you' or 'Never again in the world'. I felt deeply ashamed of my white skin, representing the western world, which in 1994 had so shamefully abandoned Rwanda to its fate. But I also felt honoured to be allowed to share in the national grief, included with all those around me as one who had also experienced the tragic loss of immediate family and friends.

This was a day of national mourning, and I had rather naively assumed the whole country would be joining the marches and ten-minute midday silence. So I was surprised to see, along the edges of the road, watching (or ignoring) us as we passed by, many other Rwandans carrying on with their daily business. What did they think of this procession? Did they struggle with the memories of the past and feel it was time to move on, not dragging the horrors back to the surface yet again? Were some angered by the emphasis on those killed in 1994 and the perceived cover-up of the reprisal killings that had happened since then? Perhaps there were even those who looked with hatred on the crowd as those who should not have escaped but should have been murdered too?

I expect the majority of those I marched with were Tutsi, as were many of those I had been spending time with recently. Some were still extremely bitter about the past, with a worrying prejudice against all Hutus, but full of praise for the progress made by the current coalition government. Others (as reflected in some of the speeches when we reached the stadium) were angry with the government for neglecting them – particularly the survivors who had been widowed or orphaned, bereft of home and livelihood, struggling for daily survival and living in fear of further killings.

In hushed conversations with Hutu friends off camera I

had heard other concerns. Examples were given to me of Hutus whose recent suspicious deaths had been hushed up, and of the excavation of mass graves that were supposedly not Tutsis from 1994 but Hutus from recent reprisal killings. Knowing how easily truth becomes distorted and how rapidly rumours spread as if truth, I tended to be sceptical of any tales reported to me. Any assessment of the current situation within the country seemed to depend on ethnic background. Suspicion and mistrust were very, very deep on both sides, and it was very hard to know who to trust or believe. I felt fearful for the future of this beautiful country.

When planning our journey we had discussed where it would be best to be for the commemorations on 7 April. The main event would be in Kigali, to be addressed by Paul Kagame, the President of Rwanda, and no doubt many other dignitaries. But Butare was where Charles had been taken, so it made sense for me to be here on this day.

Much had been made of the ten minutes' silence to be observed at midday in Rwanda, while the rest of the world was invited to take two minutes' silence in solidarity. I find silence extremely powerful, and the act of sitting in silence among thousands of grieving Rwandans, remembering our loved ones, in the town where Charles had spent his last days alive, would be the most significant part of the whole day for me.

The ceremony was due to end at midday with this time of silence. However, just fifteen minutes before midday, having rushed through the final part of the programme, it was announced that due to the gathering black clouds and imminent rain, the event was now finished and we were free to return home! I sat there in disbelief, feeling bitterly disappointed and cheated. Next to me was a university professor who was equally annoyed. It would take most of the people present much more than ten minutes to walk home, so ironically they would all be soaked in the rain anyway.

It was infuriating. I had come all the way from the UK in order to be in Rwanda for the tenth anniversary commemorations, to share these with the people of Rwanda. But now I was not able to do that. Sue and I decided that the next best thing was to stay sitting in the grandstand anyway, observing the silence on our own. But even that was not to be. The Bishop's car had arrived to collect him, and he was insisting we should be taken home before him, so we were encouraged to move quickly in order to allow the chauffeur time to come back for the Bishop before the rain came down. It would have been very impolite to refuse his kindness, so we had no choice but to pile into a couple of cars and go.

As we drove back towards the diocese, I watched the minutes ticking by on the little clock in the car dashboard. Midday was approaching and people were still chatting, apparently oblivious. 'Could we maybe have a little silence at midday,' I asked, 'just to join with others all over the world in remembering those who died?' But even that did not last longer than a few seconds. I was intensely frustrated.

Back at the diocese, as a last attempt, Sue, Apollonie and I went to sit outside the little guest room where we had slept the night before. There were two girls in the room cleaning, but they kindly agreed to leave us alone for ten minutes. At last we could be still and silent. And at last the tears, not far from the surface all morning, found freedom to fall. Despite all I had learned in the past few days about Charles, I realised I still loved him and grieved over his senseless death. But perhaps I was grieving too for the life we would never have had together, weeping over the pain of betrayal as well as the sadness of death. Maybe after the rush and pressure of our first two weeks in Rwanda, in this rare moment of calm and reflection, the roller-coaster of impressions, discoveries and fears was catching up with me and I was simply exhausted.

The silence was broken after just a few minutes by Apollonie praying. Sue followed with a prayer, but I could say nothing. As she had done ten years previously, Apollonie urged me not to cry. 'Courage,' she said gently, putting her hand on my arm. But I needed to cry, and I tried to explain to her our different cultural approach to expressing our emotion. There had been very few tears at the commemoration event, but I could not help thinking that a more spontaneous, outward expression of grief could help us all in dealing with our pain.

Lying in my bed that night I tried to figure out what was behind my confusing feelings during that memorial event in the stadium. My attention during the previous two weeks – and particularly in the stadium – had been very much on the appalling happenings of ten years ago, evoking memories of the atrocities and terror, and outrage at those who had planned and executed it with icy precision and determination. And rightly so. This had been one of the worst crimes in the past century and should never be forgotten.

But how was it for those who *were* involved but now genuinely deeply regretted it? Would they ever be able to forgive themselves and move on when living with constant reminders of the past? And what of those who were not involved but live with the guilt of not having done anything to stop the spread of the killing? I knew of Hutus who had certainly not taken any part in the genocide but who felt they bore responsibility for the actions of their fellow Hutus, extremists in the militia or army.

Were the commemorations essential as part of the healing of the bereaved and a deterrent to any future uprisings? Or would there come a time when the emphasis on the past could take a less prominent position in the interests of reconciliation and healing between the various groups? I fear that even to suggest such a thing would bring a howl of indignant disapproval from some quarters, opening myself to accusations of belittling the past and betraying the dead.

I realised my experience was very limited. I was staying in the country for less than one month and it happened to be at a very difficult time. Now, at the tenth anniversary of the genocide, there would inevitably be a major focus on the past with commemoration events all over the country and filling the media. Had I been here at another time, and with a different agenda, would I perhaps have been hardly aware of any national remembrance of the past? I confess I don't know. I long to see justice done *and* I also long to see individuals and communities healed and reconciled. The two belong together as two sides of the same coin. But before looking at the conflicts between others, I first needed to be able to deal with my own bitterness, hurt and anger. That evening, these were not far below the surface.

The next day we were going to attempt to make contact with Kabalira in prison, and I was dreading it. But there were others we would need to meet too, if possible before seeing Kabalira: survivors from the genocide who had been around at the time Charles was taken, and who might have information. The crew had given me a few names and contacts – people they had met or heard of in their previous visit. But I was struggling to know how to proceed. Jay and Ray seemed full of ideas and relevant questions to ask the people we would meet. I could think of none – not even in English, far less in Kinyarwandan.

I wrote in my journal that night:

> *At times like this I just feel like giving up. Why am I doing this? If I really wanted to know, surely I'd be pushing doors myself and doing everything to find out. But I'm not at all sure I do now. Really, what is to be gained? Then when we discuss who to see, what's been said, what to ask, etc., I can't remember what I know or who said what or when. My brain can't take in too much info. at the moment.*

I didn't sleep much that night, a combination of anxieties and mosquitoes nibbling at me from within and without.

7

Gathering Information

Left to my own devices I would have had no idea how to go about arranging to meet a prisoner. But Bishop Mutiganda was already making plans. He had been amazingly helpful to us, not only providing an empty house for us to stay in, and a young lady to cook and clean for us, but also a spare car complete with chauffeur! On top of this, he frequently changed his schedule in order to accompany us somewhere or make arrangements for us. We could not have managed without his generous help.

This morning he had arranged for us to go to the Attorney's office to request permission to see Kabalira. I had no doubt the arrangements would take most of the day to process and fully expected we would have to come back another day to see Kabalira – if we were allowed to see him at all. That might give us a day or two to track down other witnesses and talk to them before seeing him. But we had at least to begin the process.

The Attorney's office was the first in a row of doors in a long, reddish-brown brick building. All along the front of these offices was a covered area to shelter waiting clients from the torrential rain, with a low concrete bench lining the outside office wall all the way along. A couple of people sat further along on the bench, watching us with interest, while a few others wandered along outside the offices.

The reception area was small. A large wooden desk in the corner took up half of two walls, and to the front and side of the desk were doors through to neighbouring offices. A dusty computer adorned the desk, surrounded by piles of papers. In the corner an equally dusty fax machine sat on a filing cabinet. A glamorous young woman got up from behind the desk as we came in and greeted us reservedly, shaking hands politely with each of us in turn. When it came to my turn, as usual I greeted her in Kinyarwandan, chatting a little. And as usual, this elicited a wide grin of delight and much hugging. It was always a good ice-breaker. Any educated Rwandan can speak either French or English or both, but it never ceases to amaze and amuse them to meet a *muzungu* who can speak Kinyarwandan – however rusty it may be!

It was a good start, but then the first setback occurred as we stood in a little office having explained our purpose in coming: the Attorney was away for the day. There was some discussion between the receptionist and a couple of others, some leisurely to-ing and fro-ing in and out of offices while we stood around waiting, not quite sure what was happening but unwilling to ask again for fear of seeming impatient and rude. That would only hinder our request. But then, after just a few minutes, we were introduced to the Vice-Attorney, a bright-eyed, smiling and vivacious man. He listened to our request, checked through our paperwork, including the all-important official documents giving permission to film, and declared that there would be no problem. He would authorise the release of Kabalira for the afternoon and have him brought to the diocese where I could interview him. As he filled out the necessary paperwork I still could hardly believe how easy it had been. This was certainly not expected! We thanked the Vice-Attorney profusely and arranged to be back at his office by 2 p.m. to rendezvous before going to the diocese.

At 2 p.m. the office door was locked, so we sat on the concrete benches along the wall outside. Over the next fifteen to twenty minutes various staff came drifting back from their lunch breaks. A few cars drew up and left again. And then Kabalira appeared. At least, I presumed it was Kabalira though I had never previously met him. A burly chap dressed in prison-pink shorts and shirt got out of a car, closely accompanied by a soldier with gun in hand, glanced hesitatingly in our direction and disappeared into the office.

A few more minutes of waiting, and then we were invited to come into the office to interview him. Ah, but this was not the plan. For one thing, we had wanted him to be taken to the diocese because I wanted him to show me exactly what had happened, what he had seen, where he had been etc. And for another thing, it was illegal to film in government offices so this crucial meeting would not be recorded. This was a huge disappointment, after such a promising start, but the Vice-Attorney was adamant.

Eventually, however, he agreed to contact the Attorney himself, who in turn said he would need permission from the Director of Prisons in Kigali. I was beginning to think it was not going to happen, when, to my amazement, he came back to tell us that the Director of Prisons had agreed to Kabalira being taken off site! 'Officialdom' was running smoother over these two weeks than I had ever known it to do before.

We met up at the Bishop's own house in the diocesan compound, just a little down the hill from the guest-house where Charles had been. Sitting around the low coffee table were myself and Sue, Kabalira with his armed guard, the Vice-Attorney and his receptionist, and the Bishop. Standing nearby were Phil and Jay filming, Ray joining in the discussion and Bosco weighing it all up from a distance. Not exactly the private chat I had hoped for but in the end probably more useful. Although I struggled with the situation, not confident in what to ask, both the Bishop and the Vice-Attorney seemed quite at ease, throwing in some very perceptive, probing questions.

Kabalira himself seemed remarkably at ease, back in the house where he had previously lived, responding confidently to our questions. He repeated the story, similar to the one I had heard from both Apollonie and Jeannette. Yes, Charles had come to ask for a room at the guest-house, but he had asked the Bishop, not Kabalira as the others had said. During those times, Kabalira had insisted, it was the Bishop who held the guest-house keys and decided who to accept. Charles had spent his days with Pastor Philip and his wife Jeannette but slept at the guest-house.

Yes, he had seen a car come into the diocesan compound around 20 or 21 April 1994 and stop outside the Bishop's house. He had come out of his house to see what was happening and saw a man in military uniform, possibly a captain, walk with the Bishop from his house down to the guest-house. A few minutes later he saw Charles get into the car with the soldier and the car drove off. It had left in the direction of the towns of Gitarama and Kigali, but other than that he had no idea where they had taken Charles.

So far I was managing to keep up with the conversation. The others with us were saying little and leaving it up to me to ask the questions. The ground we were covering was familiar, and Kabalira was pausing to allow me time to translate for Sue. But then others began to join in the conversation. Had Kabalira ever visited Charles at all, given that they were colleagues and fellow pastors? No, he replied, he had not once gone to Charles' room because 'times were bad' and he knew Charles was at risk so he did not want to put his life in any more danger. Yet, someone pointed out, he had repeatedly visited Pastor Philip in his home, even though he knew he too was in danger.

Someone else asked who else was living in the guest-house at the time. 'There was a man who came from Kigali – Nsabimana his name was,' he volunteered immediately. 'Nsabimana Josue. He worked in the Information Service of the Presidency. He had a lot of visitors coming and going from Kigali – officials from the ministries and others.'

I was not the only one who was shocked by this news. Many government officials had been involved in planning and orchestrating the genocide, so having such people around in the compound would have been extremely dangerous for those at risk. 'So could *anyone* just come and stay at the guest-house?' the Vice-Attorney asked.

'This man had known Pastor Philip,' Kabalira replied. 'He was fleeing from Kigali and needed somewhere to stay. But he didn't stay long. When the President issued an edict that everyone should go back to work, he left.'

Now I was totally confused. If he was fleeing, presumably he was a Tutsi or moderate Hutu whose life was at risk. But why then was he receiving official government visitors? And how could he simply go back to work if he was so much at risk? Had I missed something?

It was only much later that I realised he would have been fleeing the rapid advance of the Rwandan Patriotic Army on Kigali, and that the President's command to 'go back to work' was the euphemistic term for killing Tutsis.

More than a year after my visit to Rwanda, when reviewing the videotapes of the interview with Kabalira as research for this book, I at last realised the significance of these visitors. Kabalira had said that among Nsabimana's visitors had been security men for Sindikubwabo. Sindikubwabo Theodore, originally from the town of Butare, was the interim President of Rwanda during the three months of the genocide. It was he who, on 19 April 1994, in the now infamous speech made in Butare and broadcast on national radio, condemned those who were not 'working', telling them to 'get out of the way and let us work.'

It was only a day or so after that speech that Charles was taken. If I had been wondering who had informed on Charles' presence in the guest-house, I probably needed to look no further. But unfortunately at the time I had not grasped the significance of these facts.

Kabalira mentioned others in the guest-house at the time – Esther, a local teacher, and a young lad, the son of a local pastor, brought there to hide just after Charles was taken. On further questioning, Kabalira admitted that the militia came on several occasions to extort money from Esther in exchange for her life, until she eventually fled. But the lad was taken soon after his arrival and presumed killed.

I found it odd that Kabalira seemed so unconcerned about these dreadful events and related them as dispassionately as if he were reading a weather report. Had he made no effort to protect the lives of those so clearly in danger who had sought refuge in his diocese?

'Why did no one take Charles into their house to hide him?' I asked. 'Well, all I know is he asked for a room at the guest-house,' Kabalira replied. 'He didn't ask me.'

'But yours was the only family who was not being hunted,' I continued. 'The Bishop's family was in danger. Pastor Philip's family was in danger. You knew that. Why did you not take him in?'

'We thought he would be safe in the guest-house,' he responded. 'It was kept locked and there were no other visitors there.'

What? That made no sense at all. 'But you *knew* it wasn't safe,' I exploded. 'The militia were coming regularly to demand money from Esther, and that guy Nsabimana was there with his visitors from Kigali. It wasn't at all safe!'

'Yes, but they had their own rooms,' he insisted. 'Charles stayed in his room. No one knew he was here. And you have to understand, no one trusted anyone in those days. Even a child at home could not be trusted.'

Perhaps he was right. Perhaps it had all happened so quickly, the extremist mayor taking over on 19 April and Charles being taken on 20 April before anyone had quite realised how dangerous the situation had become. Or perhaps there was more Kabalira could have done to protect him and others. Either way, I was feeling decidedly uncomfortable. Here he was, relating the tragedy of the death of his fellow pastor and colleague, knowing that he had done nothing to prevent it, yet he appeared totally indifferent about it. His dead colleague's widow was sitting right opposite him, yet he showed not the slightest inkling of remorse or sadness, and he made no attempt to offer condolences. Either prison had made him extremely heartless or he had something to hide. Despite all his protestations of innocence I wondered if he might have had a more significant role in Charles' death than he was prepared to admit to.

Before returning to the prison Kabalira went with us to the road leading to the guest-house to indicate the route the car had taken. As we talked over seemingly repetitive details his minders lost interest and began chatting a few metres away from us.

I asked him if he knew why he had been put in prison. A kind of awkward smile crossed his lips – the only smile I had seen all afternoon. 'No,' he replied, 'I have no idea. They haven't told me anything.'

'But what about you?' I pressed. 'Why do you think you've been locked up?'

Kabalira looked away, smiled again and shifted nervously. 'Well... you see, er... A lot of people have been locked up.' He seemed to be searching for words. 'They might not have done anything but they're suspected. People maybe had something against me I suppose.'

Then he asked me, 'Is it you who has accused me and had me put in prison?'

'Absolutely not,' I answered. 'I knew nothing of your involvement until a few weeks ago.'

At this point the Vice-Attorney called over to us, keen to get Kabalira back into the car and away. His time was up. As he walked back towards the car Kabalira asked if I thought he had had any part to play in the death of Charles. I told him I could not say at this stage. I was gathering information and had only small sections of the bigger picture so far. He held his hands up in the air. 'I tell you the truth before God,' he said. 'I have never killed anyone or betrayed them, or wished malice on anyone, whoever they are.' It was not the first time he had claimed his innocence as a man of God.

We shook hands and I thanked him for his time. Maybe not the most obvious way to bid farewell to the man who may have had a part to play in the death of my husband, but it just came out automatically. I'd never had dealings with a suspected 'genocidaire' before. I was left troubled after that encounter. If Kabalira had been involved, if he had been a spy for the militia right in the heart of the diocese, as others had clearly suggested, claiming to protect his colleagues when in fact he was betraying them, then that was despicable beyond words. And his sitting there denying it outright, appealing to his truthful nature as a pastor, chilled me to the bone.

On the other hand, maybe I'm just naive, but I could not blame him outright because the evidence was by no means unequivocal and his explanations did seem quite plausible. I knew of people who had accused him. But I also knew that people do fabricate and twist stories in order to seize the opportunity to get back at someone they dislike for whatever reason. I would need to gather more evidence, try to find others who had seen him during the genocide and were prepared to talk. I had somehow to keep an open mind about him.

The fact that he was a pastor no longer swayed me one way or the other. Many people I have spoken to over the years in the UK have been incredulous that pastors could have been involved in genocidal atrocities. But they were. Many of them. The Diocese of Butare alone had several pastors in prison on suspicion of crimes of genocide. Pastors are just as vulnerable to the lure of adultery and the pull or pressure of murder as any other human being. Profoundly tragic, but true.

This was another of those times when I really needed to find some space and quiet to talk over the events of the day, but it was not to be. It was the day after the tenth anniversary commemoration events, approaching Easter weekend, and Tearfund's media department had co-ordinated several requests for radio interviews. No high-tech studio, however. Just a satellite phone – borrowed from Tearfund – on the path outside the Bishop's house, and a less-than-successful attempt to put into a few words the events, thoughts and feelings of the past two weeks.

It was so good to have our own place to stay. I had the best night's sleep so far, having bought a mosquito net down town for only 2,500 Rwandan francs, around £2.50. Alodiya was happy to buy and prepare for us whatever we wanted, so I had put in a request for *sosoma* – a nutritious porridge made of sorghum, soya and maize that Charles had introduced me to. Delicious! And there were also the usual omelettes, fresh pineapple, bread and honey.

Phil reminded us over breakfast that it was Easter Friday, so before we set out for the day's business he read to us Jesus' prayer for his disciples from John 15 and we prayed together. Even if my own faith was struggling, I was grateful for the strength of the others around me. I knew God was around somewhere and I was comfortable with a sense of just 'being' in his presence, but I found it hard to trust him or put my inner sighs into words of prayer. Ray, Phil and Jay really seemed to respect that, maybe even sharing it to some extent themselves. It had been good to chat with them sometimes over our questions about God and frustrations with the church. I so much appreciated their openness and down-to-earth, practical faith.

Our first stop that morning was to see the widow of the former Bishop of Butare. I had previously met with this

bishop back in 1994 on my first trip back to Rwanda after
the genocide. It was to him that Charles had come seeking
refuge and it was he who had given Charles a room in the
diocesan guest-house. When we met in 1994 I remember
being extremely unimpressed by his responses and lack of
compassion. Why had he not done more to protect Charles?
Surely he knew he was at risk and could have taken him into
his house for safety? But later I began to wonder what I
might have done if faced with the same dilemma. What
threats might he have been facing at the time? Was he
perhaps already hiding others in his house? If the city of
Butare was still relatively quiet, was he aware of how bad it
would get? Perhaps, like Charles, he thought the violence
might calm down and that Charles would be safe enough on
the diocesan compound. I had no way of finding out because
only a few months after I met with him, the Bishop died. I
would find out shortly whether or not his widow, Doroteya,
might have anything to add.

Doroteya chose to speak to us in English, making life
much easier for me. She spoke softly and chose her words
carefully, reluctant to give too much away. Recalling the
events of April 1994, when Charles had come to the diocese,
she said it had been somewhere around the seventeenth to
nineteenth of April when the military came looking for him.
At that stage the situation had still been relatively calm in
Butare and Charles had been fairly free in his movements,
she said, even joining with other Christians in the cathedral
to pray.

From other sources I had heard that Charles had been
taken on or after the twenty-first of April, the turning point
which had seen the beginning of widespread massacres in
the area. But Doroteya was suggesting it had been earlier
than that. She told us how soldiers in a civilian vehicle had
come to the Bishop's house saying they had information that
he was housing '*inkotanyi*'.[4] The Bishop had insisted he had
no *inkotanyi* in the compound, the only recent arrival to the

guest-house being a pastor from the Episcopal Church but not an *inkotanyi*. But the soldiers apparently knew Charles' name and insisted on going to see him, alone, despite the protestations of the Bishop who wanted to accompany them.

A short time later Kabalira came to the Bishop's house to tell him that Charles had been taken. It was thought perhaps he had been taken for questioning, but given the rapid deterioration in security around the country, Doroteya told me that they feared for Charles' safety. How had these soldiers known about Charles? Where had they got their information from? By all accounts Charles had been around in the compound for several days before he was taken so he might have been seen by a number of people. But Doroteya also mentioned the arrival sometime in April of Nsabimana, a former pupil of Pastor Philip's when he had been a school chaplain. Nsabimana was later found to be a member of the *interahamwe* or militia. There was certainly a possibility that he might he have informed on Charles. But then, Doroteya was not clear on whether he had arrived at the guest-house before or after Charles had been taken.

We were picking up little snippets of information, getting the broader picture, but it was proving to be extremely difficult to get accurate details. A few other names came up again, however: Esther, a teacher who had been staying in the guest-house since before the troubles had begun, but who had escaped; Munyaneza, a child at the time who had hidden in his father's workshop on the compound throughout the genocide; and an archdeacon who had fled to the compound with his family and been hidden in a room behind the cathedral. These had all survived and were living still in Butare. It would be crucial to talk with them.

But what of Kabalira? How did Doroteya view his role throughout the genocide? She described how he came regularly to report to her husband, telling him what was happening outside, who had been taken, and who had been killed. He had warned them that their own lives were at risk.

'They want to kill you,' he told them. 'But I am here to protect you.'

But when several of Doroteya's family members fled to her house and were hiding there, Kabalira's tune had changed. 'He told us we were not allowed to hide people,' she said, her voice beginning to shake. 'He told us we must let him take them away to a safe place or we would all be killed.'

'So he was negotiating with the militia?' I asked, realising already that Kabalira must have been lying to us.

'Everyone knew that,' she responded immediately. 'I didn't see it myself because I was hiding, but he came to report to my husband every day.'

She was now not just reporting facts but reliving them, with all the rawness of the emotion and memories. It was terribly painful for her to remember.

'He said the family would have to go. He said he would take them somewhere safe, and I should trust him. My husband didn't want them to go. Me also, I didn't want them to go.' She spoke through her tears, banging her fist on the arm of the chair. 'We were ready to die together, but my family said they would go with him to keep us safe. They went with Kabalira and he didn't protect them.'

Several of them, I discovered, were killed. But some did escape. 'They saw what happened,' she whispered barely audibly, her voice trembling. 'They will tell what they saw.'

She was clearly very distressed at this memory, but would not blame Kabalira outright for their deaths. I asked what she would like to see happen to him now, but her response was noncommittal. Other people would be involved and decide how justice should be done, she said. Could she say what she thought justice should be in this situation? But she would not answer this. So, she would not accuse Kabalira, but clearly her assumption was that he was guilty. She too had met with him, and interestingly she too noted that he showed no sign of remorse or regret over the deaths of her family – as we had noticed over the death of Charles.

I came away from the meeting with Doroteya with a very different impression to that which I'd had ten years before. With a Tutsi wife and a house full of Tutsi relatives I guess the Bishop felt he had enough on his hands without taking in anyone else. There was no indication that Charles had asked to be housed anywhere other than the guest-house, and having arrived in Butare before the violence there spiralled out of control perhaps he felt there would not be any need to be hidden elsewhere.

It was around 20 or 21 April that the Mayor of Butare was replaced by a hardliner and the mass killings began – and it was around that time, or even before, that Charles was taken from his room in the diocese. There would have been no time to flee again or search for somewhere safer.

In the afternoon we began to follow up some of the other contacts mentioned to us by Doroteya and others, starting with Archdeacon Zakariya. Zakariya and his family had been hiding in a little room in the back of the cathedral throughout the genocide, and it had never been searched, so they had all survived. Why, oh why, had Charles not been hidden in there? Then he too might still have been alive today.

The Archdeacon had apparently been ill for some time and rarely received visitors. When the crew had been out in January they had met with his wife, but he himself had been through the back of the house in bed and they had not been allowed to talk with him. It had been suggested to us that this was perhaps not surprising, and that Zakariya would not want to answer questions because he had something to hide. Consequently we were all the more determined to talk with him.

We had given no prior warning of our visit, but to our great surprise we were welcomed not only into the house, but even through to the Archdeacon's bedroom where, right enough, he lay in bed. He told us he had chronic back problems, which had confined him to bed for months in considerable pain. In this small room there was only room for Sue, Phil and myself – I perched on the side of the bed, Sue had the chair, and Phil stood squashed as far back as physically possible against the wall with his camera.

Zakariya recounted his story to us. He had come to the diocese seeking refuge in mid-May, well after Charles had been taken, so he had no information about the events surrounding his disappearance. Security in the area had deteriorated rapidly by the time Zakariya had fled to the diocese, which was why the Bishop had considered it safer to hide him in the little room behind the cathedral. He confirmed my thinking that before 20 or 21 April it might not have been thought quite so essential to hide. And he also confirmed my fears that Kabalira was involved with the militia.

'From our hiding place we could see what was happening outside,' he informed me. 'He was often around with Kazungu, the militia leader in Butare. And he had a gun.'

He told us that it had been Kabalira who had brought the militia to their hiding place in the small chapel. 'We gave them a lot of money, so they didn't kill us that first time,' added Zakariya's adult son Joseph, who had been sitting in the corner throughout our discussion, chipping in occasionally. 'And then we fled before they were able to come back again.'

Neither Zakariya nor his son knew Charles at all, and having arrived at the diocese after Charles had been taken, they were not able to help with the details. 'But Kabalira would know,' Zakariya insisted. 'He'd been around in the area for years and he knew the local leaders. If you asked him he could definitely tell you where they took Charles.'

The evidence was definitely mounting against Kabalira, with the Archdeacon's testimony being particularly powerful because it was an eyewitness account. But the immensely frustrating fact was that Kabalira could not – or would not – tell us what had happened to Charles. And he had also flatly denied any involvement with the militia. So someone along the way was lying – or being economical with the truth.

Towards the end of our conversation Joseph suggested we might like to meet with a friend of his, who had himself been in the diocesan compound during the genocide, and might have information to give us. The friend, Munyaneza, turned out to be the same young man mentioned to us already by both Kabalira and Doroteya. As it happened, Joseph sang in the same cathedral choir as Munyaneza and the choir practice was that evening.

We had by this time been with Zakariya for quite a while and he seemed tired. He had given us as much information as he knew so we decided it was time to take our leave and head back to the cathedral with Joseph to talk to Munyaneza.

I was reluctant to let Joseph disturb the choir practice by bringing Munyaneza out to us, but he insisted it wouldn't be a problem. As we waited outside the cathedral, a few inquisitive onlookers gathered at a distance and eyed us up. After some time a young man emerged whom we took to be Munyaneza. We introduced ourselves and explained our purpose in coming. Had he been around in the diocese at the time and perhaps seen Charles or known anything about what had happened to him?

Several people had told us that Munyaneza's father used to have a small workshop on the diocesan compound, and that Munyaneza had hidden there himself, although only a boy at the time, throughout much of the genocide. Munyaneza, however, seemed very reluctant to talk about it at all. He didn't know anything, he told us several times. He was down the hill from the guest-house so did not see anything. But we should ask Esther instead; she would know more.

Esther, whose name had been mentioned by several people, was also a guest in the guest-house so might have actually spoken with Charles or seen precisely what had happened the day he was taken. She might also have seen whether or not Kabalira was collaborating with the militia. Munyaneza mentioned her name several times. Clearly he thought she would be a key witness.

I was disappointed that Munyaneza was so reluctant to talk, but on reflection realised that we were in a fairly public place so he could well have been anxious about anyone listening in or picking up snippets of our conversation. Or maybe he simply wanted to get back into the choir practice. At any rate, he seemed happy to agree to meet us again the following day so he could take us to the spot where his father's workshop had been and where he had been hiding. Maybe there would be more he could tell us away from the public.

It had been a strange day. We had met four potentially very key people and gleaned some snippets of new information, but actually it was not information that took our case any further forward. I was beginning to wonder if we would ever get to the bottom of what happened. Was there anyone around who had seen what happened and was prepared to tell the truth?

I was up early the next day and after washing in the bath, squatting over a basin of water, I ventured out the back of the house to see how breakfast was coming along. Alodiya was outside the back door, leaning over a charcoal burner on which she was cooking my *sosoma* porridge. A young girl sat on the edge of a low wall nearby, bouncing Alodiya's baby on her lap. Around the charcoal burner, on the ground, sat a bowl of fresh eggs, a plate with some finely chopped onion for the omelettes, and a tray with various cooking implements. It had rained heavily the night before but already the morning sun was beginning to dry up the mud. Nonetheless it still took considerable skill to cook for six people outside on mud – and produce a hot, delicious (and clean!) breakfast.

Alodiya declined my offer of help and seemed a bit flustered by my presence while she was busy, so I left her to get on with her job and wandered round to the front of the house. It was such a lovely time of day and everything felt fresh after the night's rain. I brought a chair onto the front balcony and sat for a while just letting my senses drink in all my surroundings. A great chorus of birds of every variety and on every tree or hedge sang and chirped at the tops of their voices; distant voices called back and forth; a puppy was crying incessantly at a nearby house, silenced only by the phut-phut of an occasional moped chugging past. The mouth-watering smell of frying onions – presumably for our breakfast omelettes – came drifting round the house. It was barely 8 a.m. but the strong sun on my face warmed me right inside and felt so lovely especially after all the rain we had been having every day.

There had been an amazingly dramatic storm the previous night at around 2 a.m. Sue and I had both been woken up by it. Huge swathes of lightning had lit up the night sky like daylight, flashing simultaneously with great cracks of thunder, like canons going off right outside the window. We had watched it from the window but it was awesome and frightening to be so close, even when relatively safe inside our house.

I could not help but think of what it must have been like this time ten years ago – trying to flee in the countryside but utterly soaked, lightning lighting up even the most secret hiding places in the dark. Did those who feared for their lives choose to move at night under cover of the dark and the torrential rain in the hope that the militia, not wanting the discomfort of being cold and drenched, might be less likely to hunt under such conditions? Would the morning sun, far from bringing relief and rest, actually intensify the terror and danger because of exposure to the hunters? How had it been for Charles on the road to Butare from Rwamagana through the back roads of Bugesera? Did the rain turn the roads to mud rivers, adding to fears that they might never get out safely? It all seemed such a far cry from the calm and warmth of this sunny morning. Could such terror really have happened in this very same place?

After breakfast we set off for the cathedral again, where we had arranged to meet Munyaneza. We were too early for him, but there were a few others around. The next day would be Easter Sunday, so a small team of women were scything the grass and weeding around the cathedral. I wandered over to chat with one who had stopped her work. She was a large lady, with a bright blue and green striped *kanga* wrapped around her waist, on which she wiped her muddy hands as I approached.

'So, did you get much out of Kabalira, then?' she asked me straight away, taking me somewhat aback. I suppose I had naively thought that his visit had been secret – forgetting that nothing in this culture is secret. There's always someone who sees, and the word then spreads quickly. But I wasn't going to give anything away – not yet anyway. I must have hesitated and looked a bit confused.

'You know, when you were talking with him here a couple of days ago. I didn't see it myself, but I heard about it.' This lady had a surprisingly confident air about her. She held her head high and spoke loudly. Clearly she was not at all worried about who might overhear her comments. So did she know Kabalira then?

'Know him? Ha!' She grunted with scorn as she tossed her head in the air. 'Everyone knows him and knows what he did. I saw him with my own eyes,' she went on, leaning towards me and jabbing her chest repeatedly with her finger as she spoke. 'He was going about with the militia, wearing his dog-collar. He had his Bible in one hand and a weapon in the other. I tell you, I saw him myself.'

I could barely get a word in edgeways as she spoke, but managed to ask if she had been here at the time.

'I was in my house down the hill there,' she said, indicating behind her with her chin. 'He came to get my husband. He was with the militia.' There were others around us by this time, though no one else was joining in the conversation. Yet the woman was not in the slightest intimidated by the presence of others as she spoke. She talked on a little, and then I asked her, 'If you're so sure of his involvement, would you be prepared to testify to the *Gacaca* when it comes? Would you be afraid?'

'What, to speak in front of the authorities?' She shook her head vigorously and waggled both pointing fingers energetically in front of her to make her response perfectly clear. 'I could *never* keep silent. They treated me so badly. They killed my son, a lovely young man. He was studying at the university. And they killed my husband.' As I turned to translate for Sue she began to wipe her eyes with the corner of her *kanga* wrap. 'No, I would never keep silent.'

I wondered aloud if she would be at risk of intimidation for her forthright speaking.

'Intimidation?' she retorted, again with scorn. 'Listen, I've known intimidation. A few weeks ago I was attacked in my own house. I was blindfolded in the middle of the night; my house was totally looted and then destroyed. I was left with nothing. I'm only here because the Bishop was kind to me and gave me somewhere to stay here. No. I tell you, they won't stop me speaking out.'

I had heard rumours of intimidation against survivors. So many who had been involved, even in the smaller crimes of looting and damage to property, were apparently still at large, to say nothing of those responsible for the greater crimes of rape and murder. Soon they would face justice at the local *Gacaca* courts. Obviously it would be in their interests to seek to intimidate into silence the few surviving witnesses to their crimes. The official line was to deny that any such widespread intimidation existed, but here was a prime example right in front of me. I remembered too that a speech by a survivor at the tenth anniversary commemorations in Butare stadium had called on the government to do more to protect survivors against such intimidation. Clearly it existed.

One of the most disturbing features of the genocide had been the intimate nature of the crimes – neighbour on neighbour, colleague on colleague. The victims knew their aggressors. Was it the same this time? Perhaps this woman knew those who had attacked her? But no. She said the militia had realised the danger of being recognised, so it was a gang from another part of town who had come to her and she didn't know any of them. Apparently this was the common practice these days. As she talked, Munyaneza had arrived and come over to join us.

'You want to ask Munyaneza,' she continued, pointing to him with her chin and still hardly pausing for breath. 'Ask Munyaneza. He'll tell you. And you should ask Esther too. She was here, she saw it all. I'll go and see Esther this evening in her house and find out for you,' she offered. 'Don't you go. Let me find out and I'll let you know.'

I wasn't sure why she was recommending that she go in our place, but perhaps she knew something I didn't. Anyway, Munyaneza also seemed to think it was a good idea. He had been keeping fairly quiet as the woman (who had not wanted to give me her name) talked on. But I wanted to hear what he had to say too. This had been a fascinating conversation, totally unexpected, but Munyaneza was already late for his prayer meeting and was clearly unwilling to talk in this public place, so I suggested he take us to see where his father's workshop had been and we headed off down the hill. As we walked down the path towards the workshop Munyaneza pointed out Pastor Philip's and Jeannette's house, where he had stayed at night, but his days had been spent in the workshop. He pointed farther downhill towards the main road out of Butare.

'That's where there was a terrible roadblock,' he said. 'From there they would bring people to the rough ground here at the bottom of the diocese to be finished off.' It was a large area of long grass and shrubs and there was no fence to mark off the point at which diocesan land finished and the neighbours' (or communal) land began. I remembered Kabalira insisting that no one had been killed on the diocesan compound, but now it looked as though many had been – either here on diocesan land or pretty close to it.

Away from others Munyaneza was ready to talk.

'One day a boy came to me for help. He was my brother's godson. There was nothing I could do for him, but he was in a terrible state so I had to try something. He was very ill and desperately hungry because he'd been living rough for weeks. I went to Kabalira to plead for help for him, but all he did was tell me I wasn't allowed to harbour anyone. The next day the militia came and took him away.' Once again I was hearing of Kabalira's dual role – protector of some and betrayer of others. If it were true, how could that man live with his conscience?

Munyaneza apologised that he could not be of more help to us. He knew Charles had been in the guest-house, but he knew nothing of what had happened. But again he suggested we speak to Esther. Up until now most of those to whom we had spoken had been willing to talk to us but, crucially, they had not been around when Charles was taken. The guest-house was not big. If Esther and Charles had been there at the same time then surely she would have spoken to him and, most importantly, seen what had happened on the day he was taken.

Munyaneza said he knew where she lived and he would be willing to take us there. It was at times like this that I was again so grateful to the Bishop for lending us a car and driver. It meant we could be flexible with plans – so essential on a quest of this nature.

It took us quite some time to locate Esther's house. As it turned out Munyaneza knew the area where she lived but not the actual house. It was a fairly main road, lined with stalls and shops interspersed with small houses, so there were plenty of people standing around for Munyaneza to ask. The road climbed steeply uphill and was peppered with particularly nasty pot-holes and ruts, so we could only crawl along very slowly. Eventually, after trying several different houses, Munyaneza knocked on a high rusty corrugated tin gate and disappeared inside. We waited in the car, surrounded by inquisitive kids, until he reappeared some minutes later. He jumped back into the car.

'Yep, it was Esther's house,' he reported back to us, 'but she wouldn't let me inside. She said she had a lot of visitors. She told me Rulinda had only spent one night at the guest-house and that the rest of the time he was either staying with Pastor Philippe or at the Bishop's house so she didn't see him again. She said that was all she knew.'

Munyaneza seemed to think that was the end of the story, but I was confused. Where did the name 'Rulinda' come from? Charles' name was Bilinda. And her report did not fit with all the other accounts we had heard so far. Was she sure it was the same person we were talking about?

'Whom exactly did you ask her about?' I asked Munyaneza. 'Pastor Rulinda from Shyogwe,' he replied. 'That was your husband wasn't it?' No wonder I was confused – and probably Esther too. It was hard enough to find the truth when we knew whom we were talking about, but when even the basic facts of name and home village are not accurate it was hopeless. Despite the wrong information, I wondered if for some reason Esther might not have wanted to admit to Munyaneza that she knew Charles. And I wondered, if I were to go back another time without Munyaneza, if she might have more to add, knowing that it was Bilinda from Gahini and not Rulinda from Shyogwe that I was looking for? It would certainly be worth a try. This woman was potentially the most significant witness so far, and I was not going to give up on her that easily.

Charles and me in the UK, summer 1993

Two scenes from our wedding. Top, a celebration drink during the traditional ceremonies, in Gahini, December 1992. And below, following our church wedding in Kigali Cathedral, January 1993

My late colleague and friend, Anatolie

Me with Anatolie's orphaned daughter, Liliose, in a refugee camp in Tanzania, October 1994

Part of the *Gacaca* process, Gahini 2004

A scene from chapter ten in which Sue and I met
one of the gang that murdered Anatolie

My meeting with Liliose, ten years after I last saw her in the refugee camp

Rows of skulls and clothing from murder victims at genocide memorial sites around the country serve as a reminder of the 800,000 or more murdered in Rwanda in 100 days.

Butare Prison. The prisoners are easily identified by their pink shirts and shorts

One of several interviews conducted with prisoners in Butare Prison

With Sue outside Butare Prison gates

Ukuri Kurakiza: Truth Heals

8

Frustration and Confusion

Our visit for the afternoon was one of the few that had been prearranged. We were continuing further south to Kigeme, where we had invited ourselves to visit another bishop.

I had had a great respect for Bishop Mvunabandi for many years. As headmaster of the church school in Gahini where Charles taught English he was a wise and hardworking leader and he and Charles had struck up a good professional relationship and personal friendship. During our wedding he had played a significant role and, later that year, when appointed Bishop of our newly formed Diocese of Kibungo, he selected Charles to be his diocesan secretary.

During and after the genocide, when the majority of his parishioners had fled to Tanzania and were living in abject poverty as refugees, Bishop Mvunabandi chose to reject the security and comfort many of his fellow bishops were enjoying in Kenya and returned instead to Tanzania to live beside his people and identify with them. He crammed his extended family and umpteen orphaned children into a tiny house on the edge of the refugee camps.

This compassionate lifestyle, however, earned him the suspicion of some of the parishioners who had remained in Rwanda, so much so that when the camps were emptied in December 1996 and all refugees returned to Rwanda, there were those who no longer accepted him as their bishop.

With typical selflessness and wisdom Mvunabandi chose to step down as bishop and face unemployment rather than being the cause of division within the church. And although sometime later he was appointed Bishop of Kigeme Diocese at the opposite side of the country, I still consider him *my* bishop.

It had been to him that I had turned for help when things began to go sour in our marriage and he and his wife Virginie had done their best to support us through the difficult months. I knew that our situation had grieved him and that even after Charles had left me, Mvunabandi had tried his best to support Charles.

Having discovered from Jeannette the news of the extent of Charles' affair, I suppose I wanted to talk with someone who had known him well, maybe to find out Charles' perspective, or just to hear confirmed what I had naively denied for so many months. There had been all sorts of rumours spread about Charles – one being that he had resigned from being a pastor and handed back his clerical robes to the Bishop. If that were true, then Mvunabandi would be the one to know.

We arrived as they were putting their sitting room furniture back in place and rehanging pictures on the walls having just finished painting. It was great to see them again – and their friendly, good-looking teenage children, whom I hadn't seen for some ten years. We chatted as they finished hanging the pictures – mostly of bishops – and they told us about the events and people portrayed in them. In the middle of this we were joined by an expatriate lady working in the diocese, and then a few minutes later by a whole van load of visitors from Rwanda and Uganda. This was turning out to be not exactly the quiet chat and catching up I had hoped for...

The conversation proceeded in a mixture of Kinyarwandan, Kiswahili and English as introductions continued and several of us tried to think where we might have met before or whom we might know in common – in other words, the stuff of everyday, unpredictable, relational life in Rwanda! The only problem was, on this particular day I really had no interest in chatting to a load of strangers about trivialities (as they seemed to me at the time). I had very limited time, and I had an agenda. This time I was in a *muzungu* frame of mind but I was caught in a typical Rwandan situation and could see no way to combine the two.

Eventually, and hoping that I was not being totally culturally insensitive, I called Virginie aside and explained my predicament. Would it be possible to have a few minutes just with her and the Bishop somewhere away from the others? To my relief this suggestion seemed to go down fine, and we slipped outside, leaving the others to talk among themselves. We walked a little around the house, admiring their neat and highly productive vegetable plot, the small shelter they had created for their cows, and their four-wheel-drive vehicles. They had certainly put a lot into making this place their home even though their working lives must be extremely busy. Pleasantries over, we sat on a bench outside the back door, facing the cows, and I explained what I had discovered.

Bishop Mvunabandi told me that yes, Charles had written a letter of resignation saying his marriage difficulties had made it impossible to continue his work. But that he had refused to accept Charles' resignation, instead asking his pastors in Rwamagana (to where Charles had moved) to support and help him. And although Charles had wanted to hand in his clerical robes, again the Bishop had not accepted them. So the rumours were not strictly true, although it was clear how they might have begun.

As far as his relationship with Martine was concerned, they would not be drawn. They knew she was a good friend but could not say how far the friendship went. It was not something Charles had talked to them about and seemed to be something they were not keen to talk about either. Instead,

Virginie was quick to reminisce fondly about Charles, his sharing with them as part of their family, how well they had worked together and how much their children had loved him as a big brother.

I knew how true that all was, and I suppose it was good to be reminded of this lovely side of Charles, which others knew so well. But at that moment I was again hurting from his betrayal and rejection of me, feeling very much the wronged party, and hearing someone sing his praises was the last thing I wanted. As I had expected, they could add nothing to the mysteries surrounding Charles' death, and I felt there was little point in talking through some of the information we had picked up along the way. Perhaps, had I had time alone with Mvunabandi, and had there not been visitors awaiting him inside, I might have bent his ear a bit longer. But this was not the time or the place and I was already feeling awkward about keeping them from their visitors. So we returned inside, joined the others for a snack, and then headed back to Butare.

It had been a disappointing visit. With the limited time and the need to focus on the task in hand of gathering specific information, the emphasis had once again been on me and my situation, and I had not been able to take time to find out much about their situation. I was really struggling with this constant focus on my issues. And even more so when this focus seemed to be leading us nowhere.

Back in Butare in the evening we relaxed over a meal outside in a town centre restaurant frequented mostly by expatriates. I reflected in my diary that night: '*Feels like two worlds – travelling in taxis (private), eating at restaurants, only making quick sorties into normal Rwandan life. Feels surreal – like I'm part of a detective saga, not real life.*' And, unfortunately, being a detective was not something I had any ambition whatsoever to be.

The next day was Easter Sunday. During the special cathedral service we were treated to numerous choirs of widely varying style and quality. Rwandans in general have a fantastic sense of rhythm and a great gift of putting profound Christian messages into song – almost ballad-like sometimes. Some choirs sang in several part harmony, either unaccompanied or with only a drum or two. They were lovely. Others made use of a keyboard with varying degrees of success – plastic music so loud we could barely hear the singing, whose harmonies were not matched by the voices, and which was frequently interspersed with a deafening, ear-piercing whistle through the PA system... Not a very pleasant experience!

In the afternoon we thought we'd try again with Esther to see if she might be more willing to talk to me alone. We found the house without difficulty this time, and I knocked on the door while Phil stood behind me with his camera on his shoulder. The others were waiting in the car. I was getting more used to the camera by now, and so, it seemed, were most people we met. Because we tended to arrive at places unannounced we would often be met with an initial look of hesitation or surprise, but after a few words of explanation most people tended to ignore the cameras.

But this time it was different. A youngster opened the door to me and I asked if I could speak to Esther. A few moments later a small, slim woman came striding through from the back of the house and immediately pushed the front door almost shut.

'What do you think you're doing?' she exploded in Kinyarwandan, standing behind the door, before I could even get a word in. 'Esther is not here. Who do you think you are, coming to someone's house with a camera without asking permission? Where's your permission to film in this country? How would you like it if I came to your country filming like that without permission?'

I was shocked! I'd never had a response like this before and it took me aback completely. I tried to keep my cool on the outside, but inside I was shaking! 'I'm looking for Esther,'

I explained to the lady. 'I just wondered if she could help me find out what happened to my husband.' I could almost see the smoke coming out of her ears, but I kept talking. 'I'm sorry if we've offended you, but we have official permission to film – look, we can show you the papers here.'

By this time Phil had stopped filming, having immediately grasped the situation, and was pulling out the filming pass to show her. He handed it over to her, asking me to tell her he would stop filming and go away if that was better. To be honest, I didn't relish the prospect of being left alone with this fiery woman but she clearly was not going to give me any indication of how I might find Esther while Phil and his camera were still here.

She calmed down a little, Phil left, and I was invited into the house.

'OK, so I'm Esther,' she admitted in a quieter voice, sitting herself down. 'Now what can I do for you?'

I was still shaking inside, awed by her self-defence tactics, and feeling daunted by the situation. I explained who I was, apologised for the confusion over names the previous day and filled her in on the information I had gathered so far about Charles' final few days at the diocesan guest-house. Did she remember him? Yes she did. She remembered seeing a red car coming to the diocese on 10 April. It went to the Bishop's house and then left. After that Charles came to the guest-house.

This was amazing. For the first time here was someone who was actually there when Charles arrived, remembering and reporting in detail what she had seen. She continued: 'The next morning he came to my room to ask me for a comb – if it's the same person, that is. He was a good-looking guy, obviously took pride in his appearance. Would that be him?' I confirmed it probably would be. 'He used it, gave it back to me, and then went back into his room. I never saw him again after that. He only stayed that one night and then he left.'

Left? On 11 April? Surely that could not be right. Every-one else so far had talked of his staying in the guest-house until 20 or 21 April. This was quite different, but she insisted on that point. So did she not see a military car coming later and taking him away? Did she not know anything about where he had gone? No, absolutely not. She was adamant that he stayed only one night and then left.

How intensely frustrating! Here was someone who was right beside Charles, could have seen and heard so much from her nearby room, yet her story did not match the others. Why? Had details been forgotten over the years? Was she confusing him with someone else? I now remember having heard of a young boy who had been brought to the guest-house for safety after Charles had been taken, but was himself taken after only one night there. Maybe this boy was older than I had imagined, and maybe Esther was thinking of him? Or was there perhaps some reason why she should not want to tell me more? Whatever it was, she quite categor-ically had nothing more to add about Charles. I asked her about her impression of Kabalira's involvement. She must have seen him around, surely? Again there was no hesitation. She verified without doubt Kabalira's involvement with the militia and his carrying a gun. She said she now sees him in prison where she works, tells him she knows what he did, that she saw him with her own eyes. But he continues to deny it.

This was the clearest testimony of Kabalira's involvement, and from a remarkably brave woman prepared to confront him on his actions. But actually, what help was that? So the evidence was mounting as to Kabalira's guilt, but that still told me nothing about what exactly happened to Charles. Only that if Kabalira was such an accomplished liar about his own role in the genocide, then it was possible he might also be lying about his ignorance of Charles' situation. Surely it was very likely that Kabalira knew who was responsible for taking Charles away, whether or not he himself was the one who informed on him. And until I could find out that information, I could go no further.

We were now getting to the end of our list of contacts and still had not found out what happened. Was there no one else who could help?

Back with the others at the house where we were staying I related the conversation with Esther. They shared my frustration and confusion. It was a low moment, in which probably each of us was wondering if we would ever get anywhere in this investigation. Not knowing whether people were telling the whole truth, being intentionally or forgetfully economical with the truth, or just blatantly telling lies, was getting to us all.

I find it hard to put into words the effect on me of this confusion. It was churning me up deep inside. To feel that there is virtually no one who can be trusted, that everyone has his or her own interpretation of events, whether remembered or fabricated, is disturbing to the core. Each person we met seemed so plausible while they talked to us. Each had a way of relating their memories in a highly convincing manner. But then afterwards I would realise how one account contradicted another, and no two stories matched up. And each time I would be left wondering if it was me who was the one getting confused and failing to understand.

It was probably made worse for me because it triggered off the deep malaise I felt through much of our married life: never knowing where Charles was; doubting his protestations of innocence; but also doubting myself and feeling totally helpless. But I was also beginning to realise why it was that so few people were taking the time and effort to search for the truth of the murders of their loved ones. Our primary focus over the past two weeks and more had been to search out the truth relating to Charles' murder. It had taken time and money to travel around the country – and both time and money were in short supply for the many people living on the breadline. It meant relating again and again the events of

1994, reliving it all over again with all the pain and distress this brings back. I had seen our hopes raised and then dashed again more times than I could remember. And *still* I seemed no nearer to finding out the truth. Was there any point?

But there was possibly one more glimmer of hope. Having not met the Attorney on our previous visit to his office, we had arranged to go back the following morning to talk with him. Equally disillusioned and frustrated, Jay had suggested we ask him to put us in contact with someone who had confessed to his or her crimes and was prepared to talk openly. At least this might restore some sense of what truth should be and maybe even some hope that one day others might confess honestly too.

The Attorney was going to Kigali for the day, so could only see us early in the morning. If we wanted to catch him, we were told, we would have to be at his office by 7 a.m. We were there bang on the dot of 7 a.m. He turned up at 8.15 a.m. He seemed quite preoccupied and little interested in our situation. He said he knew nothing of who had driven the car which took Charles away and did not know anyone who had confessed in the Butare area, because 'they were mostly intellectuals' – although quite what that was supposed to mean I was not sure.

However, he eventually called in his Vice-Attorney – the one who had been so helpful to us on our previous visit. In a highly respectful and gracious manner he 'reminded' the Attorney of three separate people who were known to have confessed. One was now released and living back in Kigali but he was not sure where. The other two were in prison, and one of them was formerly from the Rwandan Army. Unfortunately we would be unable to see them that day as the Attorney was to be away all day, but we were assured there would be no problem in making an appointment to see them in prison on our return in a few days. I was impressed by this Vice-Attorney. He seemed to know the local situation well and was making a great effort to be helpful towards us.

So once again there was a ray of hope. To be able to speak to someone who had been in the Rwandan army in Butare during the genocide, and who was now prepared to speak out about his crimes – he had the potential to be very helpful. If he knew the hierarchy of the army locally, which he no doubt would, then he might be able to tell us who would have been responsible for the area in which the diocese was situated. And knowing how rapidly information is disseminated and retained in this country, he might even have heard about Charles' abduction and subsequent death.

Maybe, just maybe, there was still the possibility of getting to the truth in the end. But it would have to wait a few days until we came back to Butare.

9

A Ray of Hope

It felt something of a relief to be back in Kigali. It was so much more familiar to me than Butare and it was good to have a little time to do more normal things. One of my longings was to go to the marketplace. The main market had moved temporarily, from its usual location in the centre of town out to a suburb, so unfortunately it was no longer within walking distance. But there was plenty of public transport heading in that direction.

I love the market. A vast covered area housed row upon row of individual stalls set up on long concrete tables. Almost everything necessary for basic everyday life could be bought there: all kinds of fruit and vegetables; umpteen varieties of beans and pulses; dried and fresh fish; fresh (and not so fresh) meat; cooking pots; new and second hand clothes and shoes; tins of dried milk; sacks of sugar; baskets and containers for the house; crafts for the tourists... Whatever was needed, it was probably somewhere here.

Each stall-holder had crammed as much into their allocated space as possible, building castles and towers out of tins of milk and tomato puree, boxes of matches and tea, bags of flour and sugar, or even bottles of oil. Pyramids of wild pink, yellow or orange spices lined one aisle, while huge basins of rancid white cassava flour attracted the flies in the next aisle. Here there was life, vibrancy, colour and variety.

Sue and I wandered round together through the bustle, avoiding the squashed fruit on the ground or the legs of a child patiently waiting by its mother, chatting to the stall-holders intrigued by the sound of a *muzungu* speaking their language, and trying to look knowledgeable as I selected some beans when really I knew nothing about the differences between them. We bought some more bananas – just enough to last us till we could get to Gahini where they were tastier and cheaper – a couple of big bags of passion fruit at something less than thirty pence a bag, and some of my favourite *sosoma* porridge flour.

It wasn't complete time off, however. Phil and Jay were also wandering round with their cameras, popping up here and there a row or two away from us, much to the consternation of the stall-holders. Being shouted at and angrily threatened in a strange language was not particularly pleasant for them, as I later discovered. But, unaware of this and devoid of cumbersome camera equipment, Sue and I were having fun.

Next stop was another visit to my bank. Charles and I had had a joint account, with both names on the cheques, although I had been able to continue using it myself over the years since his death. Ten years later I now felt I could at last face asking for his name to be deleted from the account. A simple little thing, but it was the last piece of official documentation which still bore his name, so it did feel like yet another step in my grieving and letting go of the ties binding me to him.

I explained my request and the reasons for it to the woman behind the counter in the small private room. She looked carefully at my chequebook as I spoke, flicking through the pages. Then she turned leisurely to consult with a couple of her colleagues seated behind, left the room for a few minutes, and finally came back.

'Because it is a joint account,' she informed me with an air of authority, 'you will need your husband's permission and signature before we can remove his name.'

Ah. Just a little bit tricky, I pointed out, again explaining the circumstances. The conversation continued, joined now by the colleagues behind her, all intrigued to quiz me about where I used to live, what I had been doing, why I had come back this time and what I thought of Rwanda now. Somehow I could not imagine having such conversations with the staff in my local bank in England! Targets, pressures and efficiency drives are so often the death of relationship and people values. But the work was being done, the paperwork completed, and eventually I was assured that if I came back the following day, my new chequebook – in my name only – would be ready for me to collect.

How often, when living in Rwanda, trying to pack too much into a short space of time, had I been stroppy in my manner and frustrated with such a relaxed attitude, finding that my impatience only slowed things down even more, in turn increasing my frustration! Now I was discovering – fifteen years too late – that a chatty, friendly, slowly-slowly approach was much more likely to elicit a helpful response, and kept my blood pressure down too! Maybe I had changed over the years. Maybe I was now more at ease with myself and less insecure than I had been. I even noticed I was much less irritated by the constant presence of little bands of barefooted, scantily clad street kids, skipping along behind us everywhere in Kigali, hands outstretched. 'Dollari! Du pain!'[5] they pleaded – keeping their options open – with pathetically sad faces. But when I stopped to chat with them in Kinyarwandan their eyes lit up and their cheeky grins returned, giving a tiny glimmer of childhood innocence all but lost through a lifetime of poverty and struggle for survival.

Yes, maybe I had changed. Or maybe it was simply the fact that being in the country for only a few whirlwind weeks was a very different experience to living here long term with all the chronic stresses and pressures that entails.

With a few minutes to spare, I popped in to see a couple

of old friends, Mr and Mrs Jan Mohammed. Of Indian origin, this Muslim couple had spent most of their working lives here in Kigali, though their adult children were now spread around the world. With so many changes around the city, the presence of their grocery shop felt kind of familiar and safe. It had expanded into the next-door shop, but not much else seemed to have changed.

'Business seems to be doing well,' I commented, snatching a brief chat with him between customers. He looked down, shaking his head and rearranging the papers on the large wooden counter in front of him. 'No, no,' he replied. 'Times are hard, you know.' It struck me that this was pretty much his response when I had last visited a few years ago – and the time before that! Would it be a bad omen to admit to any progress in the business? Maybe it was genuinely tough going. They certainly worked extremely hard, and I really admired them for their courage in sticking it out right through the troubles.

I looked around at the shelves behind the counter, packed high to the ceiling: men's shirts and children's dresses; thermos flasks, plates and mugs; skin cream and hair lotions; coffee, tea, flour, bread... their joint aroma mixing with the fumes from the street outside and the sweat of young men lugging heavy boxes around. With our return to Gahini coming up soon, it was a chance to stock up on supplies for my friends and family there – tea, sugar and powdered milk – though, being on foot with only a rucksack for shopping, I would have to exercise some restraint.

Maybe I was a little more relaxed now, perhaps allowing myself just to enjoy being in the country and doing normal things again. So, later in the day when Jay suggested we go back to the cathedral where Charles and I had been married, it seemed a fairly safe idea at the time. It was just a building, after all. And we would only be looking around.

It was only when I stepped out of the hot sunshine and into the cool of the building that I realised I had not been back in the cathedral in the eleven years since our wedding. I began to feel my stomach fluttering again – but this time not with excitement.

There were some new wall hangings at the front behind the altar and Communion table, but apart from that very little seemed to have changed. I walked slowly up the central aisle, looking to left and right at the rows of wooden pews, as memories of that same walk came flooding back to me. The Bishop had led the way in his golden robe and scarlet mitre, and as I heard the organ strike up Wagner's wedding march I had felt close to bursting with happiness.

Today there was no sound but my footsteps. Reaching the front of the church I turned to face the empty pews. Eleven years before, the church had been nearly full. At the front of the central section had sat my mum and dad, and beside them John and Gemima – my Rwandan 'parents'. The left section had been headed by my bridesmaids, the best man, and Charles' father and stepmother. Behind them sat close friends and family. And there in the middle of them was Martine. At the time of course this had had no significance for me – I don't think I even noticed her there. But eighteen months later, when I knew the rumours about her and Charles were true, and I looked back on photographs with her in such clear view, I was incensed with anger. Martine had had the nerve to sit right up near the front among close family and friends! Now... now I no longer knew what to think. It was as if the past eleven years had all rolled together in the space of a few moments. Happiness, anger, sadness, pain, crushing disappointment, despair...

I stood for a while looking around and reflecting, then sank down on the altar steps, the very spot where Charles and I had knelt to receive Communion, and buried my head in my hands. The whole jumble of emotions was again overwhelming. What was the point of all this? It just seemed to be reawakening such pain and trauma but with what benefit? I had not yet found the truth about Charles' final hours, and seriously doubted that I ever would – or even if I actually wanted to. I didn't know if I could take much more. But, as I reflected to Sue through my tears, I had discovered *some* truth – the truth about Charles' relationship with Martine. It was not at all the news I had been expecting. And it had been devastating, dashing my hopes and forcing me to face unwelcome reality. But in a strange kind of way, knowing this truth also felt quite freeing. I remembered the anger I had felt towards Martine, but I realised now I no longer felt it. I could look again at the spot where she had sat and feel, well, probably more sadness than anything else. For her, for Charles, for the way things had worked out. I thought about how my life had moved on in the intervening years, about the opportunities I'd had and how much I was grateful for now.

Discovering the truth can be shocking, but it can also be releasing. I realised this was part of the message the government in Rwanda was trying to impart to the population in relation to the *Gacaca* courts. '*Ukuri kurakira*' proclaimed huge *Gacaca* posters along the roadside all over the country. 'Truth heals.' On the one hand I could endorse that now, having realised its impact in my own life. But on the other hand, when it came to searching for the truth about Charles' murder, I knew full well that the process necessary to get there can itself be unbearably traumatic. Hundreds of thousands of Rwandans were having to make that choice in these days. Could they face putting themselves through such torment by reawakening the horrors of the genocide months? If discovering the truth could be the guaranteed end result, it might be worth the agony. But when the pathway to search for truth is strewn with lies and silence, intimidation and dead ends, and the reawakening of pain with no resolution, who would choose to follow it? Remarkably many have and still do, and for them the *Gacaca* courts have revealed details of the deaths of their loved ones, enabling them to unearth their remains and give them a dignified burial. Some killers have confessed to their crimes and there have been remarkable instances of reconciliation. Even as I write this now I have just received an email from a friend in Rwanda relating such an incident:

> Yesterday Samuel, the leader of the association, gave us a testimony on how he was able to forgive a man who was sitting next to him in *Gacaca* and stood up and confessed he had killed Samuel's older brother and gave all the details. It was for him the first time to hear that. It was so powerful, I did not find my line of thoughts when time came for me to preach. God is faithful. Please keep praying for us.

But, for others, truth remains buried with their families while the mystery and pain continue. Yet, for all that, life carries on in Rwanda. The resilience and courage of the vast numbers of women and children widowed and orphaned by the genocide humbles me to the core. How do they survive? What was troubling me, however, was not just my own personal struggles, but the worry of what might be the effect of my investigations on those I was talking to. Frustrating though it had been to have not yet found anyone who could provide the information we were looking for, many people had nonetheless been remarkably open over some issues. What was more, in this small country of highly efficient and rapid word-of-mouth communication, I could not begin to imagine who might have been watching our journeys and conversations and constructing a dossier against those who had been so helpful towards us. Or was I just being paranoid?

I was disturbed by the fact that I seemed to have breezed in, upturned as many stones as possible and pushed for information to further *my* investigation, and then would breeze out again leaving those who had helped us to cope with the aftermath. Given that I was returning to security and comfort and absolutely no risk to my personal safety, leaving friends to face potentially increased personal danger in an already volatile situation, was that not grossly unfair? Their suffering was already far greater than mine, and they had lost so much more than me, the last thing I wanted to do was to add to it. These were genuine concerns, but perhaps underlying them was also my dread of possibly having to confront the person or people responsible for Charles' death. Did I really want to hear the truth? My mind and emotions were in constant battle between knowing that the truth liberates, yet fearing to hear it.

We only had a few days left in the country and already I was looking forward to being home again, away from the ever-present inner turmoil and anxiety. But before that we still had planned a trip back to Gahini to participate in the *Gacaca*, hoping to find more information about the death of my colleague Anatolie. And also a final trip to Butare to interview confessed criminals in prison. It was always possible that either of these visits might uncover new information about Charles' circumstances. I would have to face that when I came to it. But first, there was a much more pleasant trip arranged.

Finding a narrow but flat strip of ground half way up the hill, squeezed in beside a hedge, Nicholas parked the Pajero and we jumped out. It was one of those deceptively sunny days, pleasantly hot but with a good layer of clouds shielding the sun, giving a false impression of protection. Foolishly I was wearing a sleeveless T-shirt, and we were going to be outside over the hottest hours of the early afternoon.

As we picked our way leisurely along the little path between the fields I could almost feel the stillness and silence. A few lazy flies buzzed around. Far away on the opposite hill across the valley could be heard the distant voices of children calling to one another. Perhaps they had taken the cows or goats to graze. Maybe they were on their way to collect water or firewood, or to take a meal to a relative in hospital. Nearer by I became aware of the rhythmic clunking of metal on stony soil, growing gradually louder as we continued on.

We rounded the corner of the field and headed on up the hill. And then I saw them in the distance – a group of twenty to thirty women dotted over the hillside, their brightly coloured clothes contrasting with the vibrant green of waist-high geranium plants among which they were working. Someone caught sight of us approaching, and one by one they downed tools, straightening themselves up from their back-breaking weeding to watch us struggling up the hill.

I had heard a lot about the co-operatives for widows and orphans set up by Nicholas Hitimana, and here at last we had the chance to meet some of the members. It was all quite a new venture, Nicholas and his wife Elsie having only recently returned to live in Rwanda. The Hitimanas had been friends of mine for many years. In 1995, after surviving the genocide and managing to escape first to Congo and then Kenya, and having overcome a threat to repatriate them to Rwanda at the height of the killings, Nicholas and Elsie came to live in Scotland. Through the Charles Bilinda Memorial Trust,[6] set up thanks to the generosity of friends and churches throughout the country and beyond, we supported Nicholas, an agriculturalist, through his MSc and then PhD at Edinburgh University. During their years in Scotland both Nicholas and Elsie won the hearts of so many around the country with whom they came into contact, and the temptation to stay on in relative safety and ease must have been great. But their hearts were always in Rwanda, with those who hurt and struggle, and so in 2001 they returned to their homeland with their three children.

It would be true to say that our entire trip would barely have been possible were it not for Nicholas and Elsie's very practical support. Both were busy people but nothing was ever too much trouble to do for us – booking accommodation, arranging minibuses to take us all over the country, answering our 101 questions – and now driving us into the countryside to introduce us to some very significant people.

'*Muraho, abakoze mwe!*'[7] I greeted the women as we approached. Their wary silence erupted into chatters of delight, and with grins on their faces, keeping their mud-caked arms respectfully at a distance from our clothes, they hugged Sue and me warmly, every single one of them. Nicholas introduced me as a fellow widow, explaining how the charity set up in Charles' memory supported him, enabling him to set up the project. 'So you're one of us!' one woman called out, to the obvious agreement of the others. I was humbled by their warmth and the privilege of being included so openly.

With great pride they pointed out to us the area of land which they were working as a co-operative, in one part growing beans and in another geranium plants. Nicholas had invited them to share in this work together and clearly they were very pleased to do so. It was the beginnings of an essential oil project – the first of its kind in Rwanda – in which geranium and eucalyptus leaves would be harvested, distilled and eventually turned into essential oils for soaps, candles, aromatherapy oils and more.

In the meantime, while the main focus of the project had not yet been fully realised, part of the land was being used to grow food crops. These women – and a few young men – came together once or twice a week to work on the land, and then between them they would share all the profits for their labours. Many of these women, whose husbands and possibly children had been murdered during the genocide, were Tutsis. But not all. There were also Hutu women among them. All were brought together by virtue of being widows or orphans.

We chatted for some time about where they had come from and how they had become involved in the project. And then I asked specifically about what benefit the co-operative had been to them personally. I knew these were extremely poor women, and imagined their houses to be very basic with no amenities. Whether or not their own children were still alive they would no doubt have several orphaned children of relatives living with them, stretching their meagre resources. Not only would it be a struggle to feed their families, but from somewhere they would have to find money to pay the children's school fees, and the medical expenses when anyone fell ill – which they frequently would. I fully expected the response to my question to be one of gratitude that at last they had the means to improve their lot just a little, providing a bit more security in very challenging circumstances. How wrong I was.

'You see, you need to understand what it was like before the co-operative started,' one lady began. 'We lived in fear, loneliness and darkness. We were afraid in our houses and very angry. The memories of what had happened were with us all the time, going round and round in our heads. It took away all our energy so our fields were neglected. No one had the heart to do any work.' There were nods and murmurs of agreement from others around. 'But now it's so different. At our meetings we talk about what happened and that helps us so much. We support each other and look out for one another now. Even if someone is having a hard time they'll still come to the co-operative because they don't want to let down their friends. Nicholas has helped us so much and now we've found that God is helping us too. Our darkness has gone now.'

I could feel the tears stinging at the back of my eyes as she talked. What an absolutely amazing story! What a complete transformation for these women from darkness, fear and hopelessness to courage, energy and hope again! Nicholas had told us a little about the meetings they hold as part of the project. He realised people needed to have the opportunity, not only to work together, but also to listen to each other's perspectives. Such meetings would be potentially explosive situations, but as a Hutu married to a Tutsi he and his wife had already had years of working through the prejudices and hurts from their ethnic backgrounds. And as committed Christians both felt strongly that their identity was now first and foremost as a child of God, and their loyalty was to God rather than any tribal allegiance.

But, as he later shared with us, Nicholas also carried with him a burden of responsibility for what he felt was his role in the genocide. As a Tutsi, his wife Elsie was a prime target for murder. And as the husband of a Tutsi, and a moderate thinker, Nicholas was also greatly at risk. He had done everything possible to protect Elsie and their baby son Jonathan and to get them safely out of the country, and he himself had no part whatsoever to play in the atrocities. Yet over the years that followed the genocide he felt increasingly convicted that because of his inaction, his failure to stand up openly against the killings and to challenge the descent into utter madness, he himself had been partly to blame. So now, as a Hutu working among many Tutsi widows, he has sought out opportunities to ask for their forgiveness.

On one occasion, at a prayer meeting for widows and orphans, he felt compelled to identify with his ethnic group and repent of the atrocities committed against Tutsis in the genocide. Wrapping a towel around his waist, he got down on his hands and knees with a basin of water, and washed the mud-caked feet of the women and orphans – a profoundly moving, symbolic and practical action for these hurting women and young people.

Challenged by Nicholas' example, and by his message of the love of God, many of these people had themselves chosen to trust God and found new purpose for living. And in turn, seeing the remarkable changes in these women, others had come asking to join the project! As well as the psychological and spiritual transformation in the women, the project was also bringing local benefits. Nicholas had discovered that where geranium was being grown, the population of malaria-bearing mosquitoes had been significantly reduced. With malaria being a major cause of illness and death in many parts of Africa, this finding could have far-reaching implications. So far he had only anecdotal evidence, but he was planning to do some scientific studies to prove the benefits. I was really impressed. As far as development was concerned, it could hardly have been more holistic. The transformations were taking place physically, psychologically and spiritually, benefiting not only the individual and the community but also the environment. A gentle, humble man, Nicholas was passionate about his work and thrilled by the developments so far. There was still a lot of work to do in developing the distilling process, but the potential for growth and development in other parts of the country was great.

This, surely *this*, was the hope for the future of Rwanda. After so much despair and hopelessness, wondering if there was anything good in this country, now I could see that there was! If change could take place so profoundly in small pockets like this, then why not on a wider scale?

As we left the women to finish their weeding, they told me I was to come back another time and join with them in their meetings. 'We belong together,' they told me. 'You don't need to be on your own. We're here to support you!' I knew they meant it and it almost brought me to tears – that sense of solidarity with the women here who understood my grief. Women who had lost so much more than I had and whose daily lot was so much harder than mine, and yet who were willing to embrace me, a foreigner, as one of their own. This indeed was a land of contrasts.

Nicholas had others for us to meet. The following morning after breakfast he popped in briefly to join us with a friend, Beatha. Beatha had wanted to share with us her story, but as she began to talk in English she became tearful, struggling to find the words to express herself. Knowing her well, Nicholas continued in English, but then she picked up again herself, more at ease in Kinyarwandan, while Nicholas translated for Sue.

Beatha herself had been hidden in the house of a militia

leader, together with her youngest child. She described how he used to come home in the evenings covered in blood.[8] Her other seven children had remained in their own house, well hidden. In time, distraught with anxiety for her children but unable to go out herself to see how they were, she asked someone to go and check on them. She told him exactly where they were and how to find them. He returned saying they were all dead, that he had seen the daughter lying dead on the street. Utterly beside herself with grief, and feeling she was losing her mind, Beatha left the house where she had been hiding and went onto the street with her youngest, wailing like a mad woman. At the first roadblock she came to, she assumes the militia must have thought she was a Hutu woman because they completely ignored her. At the second roadblock she told them she was going to the house of the leader of the militia to be killed. 'I just wanted to die,' she told us, clearly still deeply distressed at the vivid memories.

Her words triggered my own acute memories of exactly the same suicidal wish. I remembered how, back in 1994 at the height of the genocide, when the news broke that the United Nations was pulling all but a handful of its troops out of Rwanda, I knew that this would be the death warrant for Charles and my final remnant of hope blew away in the tailwind of their retreating planes. I felt there was nothing, absolutely nothing, left to live for. Not that I wanted actively to take my life, but I really hoped that some accident might end it quickly for me. But for me it was 'only' (as people have said to me) my husband, whereas Beatha was talking of the death, not only of her husband, but also of almost all her children – and that possibly through her rash informing on their hiding place. I could not even begin to imagine the sheer torture this must have been for her.

She managed to reach the militia leader's house, finding his wife there. Far from killing Beatha, she took pity on her and hid her with her child, and somehow in this way she survived. Now, years later the wife is in prison but Beatha has been to see her and testified publicly to her innocence. Sometime later Beatha heard the news that one of her children was in a refugee camp in Goma, on the Rwanda–Congo border, having been rescued by the girl who had been helping them in their house. Then she was told of a third child who had hidden in an orphanage run by Catholic priests and was about to be taken to Italy as an orphan. She has now been reunited with both these children – but of the other five she had no news and only discovered what had happened to them when their murderer confessed to their killings.

Beatha is trained as a teacher, so after the genocide she found a job teaching in a school. 'But I was so angry about what had happened,' she explained, 'that I just could not face looking at Hutu children in the class. So I had to leave my job.' She took a job in a bank instead, but was having difficulty concentrating and could not sleep at night. A colleague told her of the organisation Nicholas was working with, suggesting they might be able to help. Beatha approached them, requesting help to be able to sleep. 'But when they talked to me and asked me questions I got really angry,' she shared. 'I didn't want that. I just wanted to be able to sleep!' However, they persevered with her, praying for her, and for the first time in years she found herself able to sleep.

Over time she began to accept the love of others and of God, and found her bitterness and anger gradually melt away. Nicholas was key in her realisation that there *are* Hutus who can be trusted and whom she can call friends, and that forgiveness *is* possible. Certainly, as she spoke she did not give the impression of being a bitter woman any longer, although having heard her awful story, the worst any mother could have to face, I would have perfectly understood if she were. But what shone beautifully through Beatha was her profound gratitude and love for God, and her passion for other widows who struggle as she did. And also her great respect for Nicholas. 'We love Nicholas,' she told us with a great smile. 'He's like Jesus,' another widow and friend of Beatha had told us, 'because he left the glories of Scotland to come back to identify with us!' And nothing either we or Nicholas could say would change her mind!

Later that day Sue and I talked more with Nicholas about the future of the Charles Bilinda Memorial Trust. Ten years on, was the priority still that of support through education and training, or had the country moved on? Over the years we had supported many Rwandans through colleges and courses in Kenya, Tanzania and Rwanda and it had been great to meet some of them at an evening event organised for the Trust a few days previously. But during these past few weeks we had also come across a number of other situations – not primarily educational – where clearly even a small amount of backing could go a long way. A single mum living at home, whose parents had both died of AIDS and who was responsible for her elderly grandmother, younger siblings and small children, for whom a £60 sewing machine could provide employment opportunities while still leaving her available to her dependants. A young man desperate to complete his studies so that he could find decent employment to support his wife and family, but unable to do so because his wife's painful chronic gynaecological condition prevented her from working to earn money to pay his fees. Yet a £30 operation could cure her completely and radically turn around their future prospects. And these were just some of the situations we ourselves had come across in a few weeks. In Nicholas and Elsie's wide network of contacts the needs were vast. But pouring in money, however well intentioned the donors, can be patronising and demeaning, taking away dignity and creating dependence. It would be essential to find ways, as Nicholas was doing, of facilitating supportive, interdependent communities, able to build on their own resources with dignity and respect. There were many larger non-governmental organisations already doing just that, but we had the advantage of being small and having direct personal contacts.

I was excited as we talked. It was almost as if something dormant were waking up within me. After a number of years during which my emotions had subconsciously dictated that I keep my involvement in Rwanda to a minimum, it felt as though my passion and compassion might slowly be coming back to life again. And after a few weeks of disillusionment, frustration and disappointment I was beginning to believe again that there might be hope.

10

Discoveries in Gahini

The *Gacaca* in Gahini was meeting every Thursday. As this was our last Thursday in Rwanda, it would be my only opportunity to attend a *Gacaca*, and to see it in action. I knew it would not offer any clues on Charles' situation, but if my late colleague Anatolie was on their list of victims to be investigated then I just might find out something more about the circumstances around her death.

With the *Gacaca* scheduled to begin at 10 a.m. we would have time to pay a return visit to the house where Charles and I had lived. It was now occupied by a German doctor and his family – Gunther, Irene and their young daughter Janine – who had been amazingly patient and accommodating with our repeated changes of plan. Today the crew wanted to film me returning to my old house, looking around and reminiscing over our year there together. There would be just time to fit that in before attending the *Gacaca* – if all went according to plan, that is...

'Our' house had belonged to the hospital, having been built for a previous doctor many years before. It was a substantial red-brick villa with low corrugated tin roof set in a sizeable plot of land. Most of the ground around was laid out to course grass, but our gardener had done amazing things with it, turning one section into a patchwork of exotic flowers of every colour and variety, and another into a productive vegetable patch. There were a couple of mature avocado trees by the front steps, and a few small papaya trees dotted over the grass.

If I stood by the festooned pillars at the top of the steps, with my back to the spacious open front balcony, the view ahead looking down the hill was awesome. My gaze took me over the hedge, down across small fields and scrubland, over the rooftops of the school buildings, along the winding road leading eventually to Uganda in the north and to layers of rolling hilltops, beyond which, to the west, lay the capital Kigali.

The two neighbouring houses, being slightly further round the side of the hill, and having been built much earlier, when the first missionaries had arrived and had first choice of location, also looked over the lake. So they could add the fiery red-orange setting sun reflected in the water to their vista – and even, on an exceptionally clear day, the snow-capped tips of the Virunga Mountains in the far north-west of Rwanda, home to the famous mountain gorillas.

It had been quite a privilege to begin our married life in such a desirable location, rattling about in this sizeable three-bedroomed house. I wondered how it would look now, having had a succession of different occupants over the years, beginning back in 1994 with the area leader of the Rwandan Patriotic Army (RPA).[9]

We walked through the gateway, now devoid of gate, following the red earth path as it swept round towards the front of the house. Phil and Jay stood back, hoping to catch some footage of me knocking on the front door and going into the house. As I approached the front steps I noticed a woman by the front door, bent double over two very large plastic basins full of soapy water.

Having heard our voices, the woman straightened up from her washing, quickly wiped her hands on her apron and turned towards me, grinning from ear to ear. It was Edissa, a young local woman who had worked many years ago for my first neighbour, an Australian physiotherapist. Amazed to find her here, and suddenly forgetting all plans to knock sedately at the door, I hugged Edissa and stood for a few minutes on the front porch listening as she filled me in on her current situation. Knowing that she had suffered from health problems and a difficult home situation over the years, I was delighted to learn that she had again found employment. And clearly she was happy in her new role.

Eventually I remembered the original plan and knocked on the front door. However, by this time Phil and Jay had long stopped filming, and were standing patiently by, coming to terms with yet another unpredicted incident that had altered their plans. Their good-natured flexibility was quite amazing! A carefully planned shot of my spontaneous arrival at our old house was obviously no longer going to happen, and the chatting on the doorstep, now joined by Irene, meant that there was insufficient time left to film inside. Ah well, we would just have to come back later – which Irene happily agreed to – and instead wander up to where the *Gacaca* was due to take place.

I was unsure of the location of the meeting, only that it would be somewhere near the church. But seeing a small group of eight or nine people each carrying a chair and making for a patch of grass opposite the church, I guessed this might be the beginning. I had expected to see possibly a couple of hundred people gathering, so I realised we must still be really early – even though it was nearly ten o'clock. Never mind. While waiting it might be useful to chat to those already here and find out more about the *Gacaca*.

The small group had arranged their chairs in a circle and each person had a file of papers they were flicking through as I approached. I shook hands with each one in turn, then introduced myself, explaining why I had come. Would the *Gacaca* be taking place here, I asked, and would it be possible for us to film part of it?

Yes, I was told, this was part of the *Gacaca* but they were

only expecting two or three more people. The big meetings –
at which witnesses give evidence and prisoners are called to
respond to the accusations – had long since passed. This was
now another phase in the process. The small group of people
gathered here was a team of leaders with responsibility for
deciding the category of guilt for each accused.[10] We were
welcome to stay, but they felt it would be neither interesting
nor relevant for us to see.

Leaving the others to begin their discussion, the leader of
the group, a pleasant-faced man by the name of John, stepped
aside from the circle and asked if there was anything he
could do to help us. We were standing under the shade of a
large tree, John was leaning on his bicycle and a few passers-
by had stopped to join in the conversation. It was a good
opportunity to find out more about the process of the
Gacaca, but also to raise a specific query. Did he know of
anyone who had confessed to their crimes and who might be
willing to talk to us?

Yes, there is one who lives very nearby, he said. 'His
name is Higiro. In fact, you might know him.' It turned out
that I did, vaguely. Or, rather, I knew his late mother, a
midwife in the hospital, and his father who had worked at
one of the local secondary schools. But Higiro himself was
not someone I particularly remembered. A bystander was
despatched to find him while we stayed talking under the
tree.

Knowing that he might well not be at home, or even if he
were, that he certainly might not want to talk to us, I was
quite surprised when only a few minutes later Higiro turned
up. A tall, bearded man, he approached us slightly hesitantly,
apologising for the delay as he had in fact been working in
his field so had taken a few minutes to wash. Over the next
few minutes various conversations were taking place in the
little crowd that had gathered around us and I found myself
talking to Higiro.

'What is it you wanted to know from me?' he asked a

little impatiently, presumably keen to get back to his work. 'Your husband wasn't in Gahini at the time so I can't give you any information about him.' I knew that, I replied, and that was not the reason I had asked to see him. Rather, I was concerned to know what had happened to my late colleague and close friend Anatolie, the wife of Ntaganda. And knowing that he had made a confession I wondered if he might know of her situation and be able to tell me honestly.

'Oh, I can tell you that,' he responded without a moment's hesitation. 'I was in the group that went to her house. We were looking for Ntaganda but he wasn't there. Anatolie came to the door and Munyemana just picked up his machete and sliced her neck. She died straight away, just one blow. Her little girl was...'

I felt the blood drain from my face and for a moment thought I would be sick. Higiro was still speaking but I was barely listening. Beside me, Sue of course could not understand a word Higiro was saying and around me others were chatting away happily, completely unaware of this sickening news I was hearing. I had a sudden urge to yell at them all, 'Would you all shut up! Don't you realise what this man is saying?' How could I politely butt into others' conversations with such unutterably horrific information? Instead, with my head spinning and staring at the ground in shock, I turned to Sue.

'I've just been told how Anatolie was murdered,' I managed to mumble. 'This man was there when it happened.' No doubt Sue was as shocked as me, but somehow she alerted the others and the conversations immediately ceased. Higiro, however, realising he was now the focus of attention, also stopped talking. And when the crew began pointing their cameras on him, asking him if he could repeat what he had just said, he looked really anxious and backed off significantly. There followed some discussion, helpfully mediated by John, as to whether he would be willing to be filmed giving his story. Not that I was paying much attention to it.

Sue and I had drawn aside a little and I was trying to put into words what Higiro had just told me while struggling to hold back my tears. Knowing Anatolie's house, I could picture the situation exactly. Did she realise what was happening? Did she have time to feel the terror? He said she had died instantly, but what of her little girl, Liliose? She was right there with her and had seen it all. The sick feeling in the pit of my stomach that I had felt back in 1994, when I first heard the news of her death, was back with me again. I had not been expecting this – and certainly not to hear these details in such a sudden way.

Yet, having come straight out with the news of Anatolie, Higiro was now extremely cagey about saying any more, looking furtively around him as if he feared others may be listening – as of course they were. To find a little more privacy we began walking down the hill towards some buildings – now empty and crumbling – which used to house Gahini Primary School.

It transpired that it was not the idea of being filmed which bothered Higiro but being seen talking on camera in a public place. John explained, as we had heard so many times before, that there is sometimes intimidation of witnesses who are prepared to speak out, so he would not want to be overheard. But if we could find somewhere a little more private he would be willing to tell his story.

Walking between two dilapidated classrooms in the row of school buildings someone suggested using a large, open room along to our left. The back wall and the back half of the side walls were solid brick covered with mud now crumbling off, while the front half was open, all covered by a rusty corrugated tin roof supported by several brick pillars. There was no furniture in the classroom, only a scratched old blackboard attached to the back wall – in fact, the very blackboard Anatolie and I had used back in 1990 when teaching in this very room. In a stroke of tragic irony here we were, about to hear a confession from someone directly involved in the death of Anatolie, in the exact same location where she and I had launched our AIDS prevention programme for primary-school children. In the far corner had been our makeshift puppet theatre, and on that same blackboard we had used a simple but fun noughts and crosses game to test their knowledge.

As with so many other scenes from my life here, I could picture exactly how it had been. I could hear Anatolie's confident voice and see her laughing eyes as she put all her energy into a lively presentation to communicate the dangers of AIDS to the innocent and not-so-innocent children before her. She was a remarkable woman. But now she was dead.

Higiro was leaning against one of the side pillars. I explained to him the connections with this classroom and he nodded, though he said nothing. Having heard the details of Anatolie's death once I had no desire to hear them again. But because the first conversation had been impromptu it had not been captured on camera, so the crew wanted Higiro to repeat what he had already told me. That was hard.

Higiro began with the events of the first days of the genocide. Following the death on 6 April of President Habyarimana and radio announcements saying 'our parent has been killed' a rumour quickly spread that he had been killed by the Tutsi rebels. The next day the local community leader had gone to the nearby local government building to fetch supplies of weapons.[11] That evening, on 7 April, after a meeting in the tiny village centre of several key local leaders whom I had known well – and trusted – the local community leader had ordered everyone out of their houses, distributed the weapons, and ordered them to go and kill Tutsis.

'You remember where Anatolie lived,' he continued. 'It was very close to the village centre so we began there. We were looking for Ntaganda. Anatolie had been out the back of the house preparing the evening meal, but when she came to the door and told them her husband was not there,

Munyemana raised his machete and gave one fierce blow on her neck.'

As he spoke, Higiro raised his right arm and swung it back down in front of him as easily as if he were scything grass. Then he put his hand to my neck to show exactly where she had been cut. As if I needed any more explanation.

'Her little girl was also cut, across her fingers I think,' he said, using the edge of his right hand to saw back and forth across the fingers of his left. 'But she didn't die.' In fact, I knew from my former doctor colleague that she had also been badly cut on the neck but he had managed to suture her wound. It was extremely remarkable that she did not die – but little wonder she had appeared so deeply traumatised when I had visited her and reminded her of her mother.

'But *why* did you do it?' I asked, unable to get my head around the fact that ordinary, decent blokes should suddenly turn into fanatical murderers. 'What had she ever done to harm you? She was a good woman; she worked hard to improve the life of the people of Rwanda. What had she done to deserve this? It just makes no sense to me.'

He thought about it for a moment. 'You're absolutely right,' he said slowly, sadly. 'Her death was unjust, senseless. She died for nothing. Even us, after we'd killed her and buried her, we were sad. Honestly, no one had anything against her. It was the gang mentality in those terrible times. I had nothing against her,' he repeated. 'She was a good woman.'

'Then *why*?' I asked again. 'What got into you to make you want to take part in this madness?'

'For many of us it was not a question of killing because we hated but because our family's life was at risk,' he began to explain. 'You see, my father is a Hutu but my mother was a Tutsi so we were threatened too. If you're from a mixed family what do you do in time of war? You go with the stronger side, not the side that's being hunted.'

'But some people did resist,' I countered. 'Some even

took Tutsis into their homes to protect them.' Higiro took my arm and gestured as if to pull me over to one side. 'Listen,' he said. 'I could take you and hide you, because you are my friend.' Then he swung his arms in the opposite direction away from me. 'But then I could go and kill others. That's what I did.' He gave me names of several people he had hidden in his house, people who are still alive today. They were names I knew and they were still living locally. I could easily check out his story if I wanted to, but I did not doubt that he was telling the truth. 'People had all sorts of reasons for being involved, you know. There were those who went with the murderers out of choice, those who went because they were forced to, those who just went to watch.'

There was a pause, and then he resumed the recounting of events. 'After the little girl had been cut we took her up to hospital and...'

'*You* took her to hospital?' I asked, incredulous. 'Why kill her mother, attack the daughter, and then take her to hospital? It makes no sense!'

Higiro was patient with my questions. I had never before had the chance to get inside the mindset of someone who had been involved in the killings and I was struggling to make any sense of it. But Higiro was doing his best to answer honestly and clearly. Perhaps he too realised the senseless-ness of the events.

'It was different in different places,' he replied. 'Some-times the gangs resisted altogether and refused to kill. At other times they told the kids to run away so they would not be killed. There was no logic to it.' No logic. Senseless. Unjust. Here was a confessed criminal looking back on those one hundred days of utter chaos and anarchy, trying to explain the inexplicable. But in his readiness to speak out and confess was he not afraid of repercussions? Might there not be those who would try to silence him, I asked? He shrugged his shoulders. 'So what. Let them kill me. Others have died. Am I better than them? I'm not afraid to die. You see,' he continued, 'after the war when I was in prison, I realised how wrong I had been. The memories were going round in my head again and again like a film – seeing people being grabbed, an arm chopped off, people lying on the ground. So I confessed to what I had done. That was years ago. I didn't confess recently with those who only confess to get out of prison.[12] It was years after my confession that I was released from prison.'

I had often wondered how I might respond if I were being pressurised to commit murder to save my own skin. Would I have found the strength and courage to resist? I hoped so. But what if I were told that my spouse, my child or my parent would be raped, tortured and killed if I did not participate? I could barely bring myself to imagine it, yet this was the impossible choice that many had had to make.

I was torn. In front of me was a man who had gone along with the murder of a very dear friend of mine and for that I despised him from the very depth of my being. Yet here in front of me was also the very same man, who had faced an unbearable decision in his family life, who now clearly regretted the past and had the guts to say so. Was there not some tiny part of me that could put myself into his shoes and feel a grain of compassion for him? For a few moments no one spoke. Then, from behind me, where there had been silence throughout our conversation, I heard Ray's voice gently ask, 'Does forgiveness feature here at all?' It was unmistakably Ray, but was it also perhaps a challenge from God? In all my theorising about forgiveness over the years, was this not now the acid test? But could I bring myself to utter the words 'I forgive you'? And anyway, did I have the right to, given that Anatolie was not my own flesh and blood, and for all I knew her own family might not choose to forgive?

I continued staring at the floor, my mind and emotions in turmoil. Higiro, of course, had not understood the comment. 'So, er, are we finished then?' he asked. I shook my head as

I continued to try desperately and string some words together.

'Anatolie was a very good friend of mine,' I began slowly, struggling to speak. 'When I heard of her death – I was in Kenya at the time – I was very, very upset. She was a good woman.' Higiro was listening carefully, his expression conveying some sympathy with what he was hearing. 'I am not part of her family so I cannot speak for them,' I continued. 'But as one of her friends…' I paused, still unsure if I could go ahead. 'As one of her friends, if I were to say that I forgive you for what you have done, how would you respond?' I searched his eyes for a response. He thought for a moment.

'I have confessed to everyone,' he began, hesitantly. 'I have spoken to those who knew her and have asked for their forgiveness. Had I known you were her friend, and had you still been living here I would have come to you too to ask for your forgiveness. Now that you have offered to forgive me, well, you know that means a lot to me.' A smile spread over his face and he held out his hand to me to shake. 'Thank you. Thank you very much indeed.' I took his hand with my right hand while wiping away a tear with my left. It was a huge relief that he had responded so positively, but I certainly didn't *feel* particularly forgiving. But then I knew enough about forgiveness to realise that it is not about nice feelings but more about a decision of the will. And that even having taken this first step, I would probably have to offer forgiveness again and again – at least in my own mind if not face to face. In the future, my memories would no doubt again trigger anger and pain.

'I didn't know that I had wronged you,' he continued. 'But now we have met and talked together we can be reconciled. God has forgiven me too, I know. That's why I'm no longer afraid.'

I turned to Sue and translated what he had just said. '*Imana ishimwe!*' she responded in Kinyarwandan. 'Praise God!' Higiro took her hand and shook it warmly, still smiling broadly. 'Long ago, if someone committed a crime against another, then the family of the victim would hate the person responsible. But I see she has forgiven me. That makes me happy.'

Later, after we had finished the interview and were wandering back up towards the road, Higiro turned to me. 'You don't know how much this means to me,' he said. 'Whenever we meet again you won't hold this against my any more, will you.' It was more of a statement than a question, but he was right. I had tentatively offered forgiveness and he had accepted it with gratitude. There was no going back now. For me the implications of this were painfully obvious, and in the back of my mind was a question I would rather not face at this point. If we did finally find those responsible for the death of Charles, would I ever be able to forgive them?

Higiro had told me where Anatolie had been buried. It was not far behind the church, on a piece of scrubland that had been turned into a mass grave during the genocide. But it had also been the site of the old village graveyard for many, many years and so could not be excavated. Those tossed like banana skins into a pit in 1994 now lay alongside those buried in peace and respect. It was also where Anatolie's six-year-old daughter Mireille had been buried, having died of malaria only two months prior to her mother's murder.

Now that I knew roughly where Anatolie lay, I felt I wanted to visit the graveyard – to pay my last respects, I suppose. But I didn't want to go empty handed. So after saying goodbye to Higiro and thanking John for all his help, we returned to our old house to ask Irene if we might pick some flowers to lay somewhere in the graveyard. The same patch on which we had grown flowers ourselves all these years ago was still awash with colour; so I selected a small bunch and we walked slowly back up the road towards the church.

There was little to suggest that the expanse of rough grass

and shrubs at the side of the road was a graveyard. There were no flowers, virtually no headstones, and a small herd of goats was wandering freely munching the grass. But I knew it was the same place where we had come to bury Mireille. It was quite a large area, and with no particular landmarks it was impossible to remember exactly where Mireille had been buried. And of course I had no idea which bit had been the mass grave where Anatolie now lay. So I picked my way over the uneven ground, far away from the road, choosing a spot under a prickly bush to lay my bunch of flowers in the hope that the goats might not eat them. My heart was very, very heavy. Ten years had passed since Anatolie's death but apart from a few brief visits back here I had spent most of those years in the UK, where my life had largely been divorced from my experiences in Rwanda. Now, back in my adopted home village, hearing afresh of the death of my late friend and colleague and visiting her grave for the first time, it brought it all back to me afresh, as though it were yesterday.

Having laid my flowers under the bush, I stood back for a few minutes, numbed yet again into silence. Sue was by my side, her arm around my shoulders conveying greater compassion and solidarity than eloquent words could ever have done. There were no words.

After some minutes we headed back across the scrubby grass and set off up the road, leaving the village behind us. We were going to visit Vasta, Gemima's mother. The short walk between the graveyard and 'Granny' Vasta's house allowed me only a brief transition and refocussing of my thoughts between the past couple of painful hours and the fun and laughter of a house full of teenagers and children. Again I thought how much easier it would be if I did not have to pack everything into such a short space of time and could have come back another day to see Granny's family – but that was not possible. Having been thwarted in our first attempt to film back in the house where Charles and I had lived, and having arranged to return in the afternoon, we had only time for a brief visit. And, again, conversation was often stilted because of the need for me to translate and act as the link between my 'family' and the crew. It was frustrating. Granny was frustrated too. We had not really talked of anything in depth, and this would be our last visit to Gahini during this trip. I felt awful having to leave them – as I did trying to explain to other friends I met along the road that I would not even have time to visit them once. Fancy coming all that way from England and not even popping in just once! I expect they thought I didn't care about them any more, although I did hope they could understand the limitations of my situation.

Since leaving Rwanda in March 1994 I had visited our house on each of my return trips into the country. On the first occasion, I was told in no uncertain terms that it was in a military zone and therefore completely out of bounds. I guess I was somewhat foolhardy to attempt to visit it – especially as I was on my own. But it turned out to be prohibited only because the military leader who had told me so was living there himself! When he reluctantly invited me in I remember being surprised to see a remarkable number of our possessions still there – presumably because it had been taken over very quickly before the looters could completely strip it. During an almost surreal conversation with this man I had tried to negotiate removing some of our furniture, not because if was of any use to me, but so I could pass it on to my in-laws, whose own house had been looted. I would rather that they had it than that it was left here to whoever happened to move in or loot further. But the discussion had turned sour and I was told that nothing belonged to me any more. As the occupant of this house for the past six months this military leader was now the rightful owner of everything here – or so he told me. I had not been interested in taking *things* home with me at the time. The loss of life – the loss of everything – had been so overwhelming that material goods seemed completely insignificant. At one point in the conversation, when the occupant had initially been more amenable and suggested I take one thing as a souvenir, I remember I had looked around in despair. Every single thing around me had a memory of some sort. How on earth could I select? It was then that I felt I'd rather not take anything – all I had wanted was Charles' life back again.

A few years later, when I again visited the house, it was occupied by the Rwandan (civilian) medical director of the hospital, and virtually everything of ours had gone. Virtually, I say, but not quite. Because over in the corner of the dining room, cracked and extremely dusty but hanging where it had always been, was our wedding *igisabo*. This was an enormous gourd, traditionally used to make a kind of butter, and an essential part of the bride's *ibirongoranwa*.[13] It was of no use to him, the doctor told me, and I was welcome to take it – which of course I did. By this time I was glad to have a link with the past – particularly one that had been so significant to our married life. But being a very fragile item, and probably some two feet in diameter, it would have been madness to attempt to take it safely home to the UK. So I entrusted it to my 'parents' John and Gemima, who lovingly cleaned and oiled it and had it mended.

This time the visit would be different again. Irene very kindly allowed us free reign over the whole house, even into the bedrooms, where of course I had not been for ten years. The place had changed a lot: the walls were painted; the furniture was arranged differently; they had their own pictures and hangings around the rooms. They had very definitely given it their own particular stamp and it felt very homely. Some things had not changed though: the gentle creak of the wooden door swinging open to the corridor by the bedrooms; the view through the wide window in 'our' bedroom past the avocado trees and down the hill; the faint smell of bats' droppings from above the flimsy ceilings. And was it my imagination or was that still a mark on the wall where we had caught a rat behind the wardrobe in the middle of the night and Charles had finished it off with his spear? This had been our bedroom, with a wonderfully wide wooden bed in the middle there. Next was the spare bedroom – but where I would come and sleep sometimes when Charles' snoring kept me awake, or latterly when I was so angry with him I could not bear to sleep in the same bed. And the last bedroom was where Charles' teenage nephew had slept and studied for school. I felt bad when I thought back to his time with us. It surely was not easy for him but he had been remarkably adaptable and good-natured. I wished I could have done more for him, but there was too much else going on in my life at the time.

Sue and I stood at the door of the tiny bathroom, and I remembered that the last cuddle Charles and I had shared had been on that very spot – a time when I thought there was again some hope for our marriage. It had been early February 1994, and we were interrupted by a knock on the back door. Anatolie's husband had come from the hospital to pass on the tragic news that their elder daughter Mireille had just died. It felt as if that day was the beginning of the end.

So many memories in this place. So much optimism and excitement in the early days but so much loneliness and pain at the end. How naive and idealistic I was in my expectations of marriage. How confusing I must have been to Charles with my mood swings, and hurtful in my patronising self-righteousness. He may have been the one to continue an extra-marital relationship, but I must have been unbearable to live with at times. It was too late now. My idealism had been shattered. We had both made so many mistakes and had been robbed of the chance to work them through and move on together. That would never be. But for me life had moved on. As I sat on the front steps looking far beyond to the hills, I realised that this was no longer my home. That might sound like an obvious statement, given that I had not lived in this house for over ten years. But I realised that

throughout those ten years a very significant part of me had
never left Rwanda. Perhaps it was because so much had
happened during my years here that had changed me forever;
perhaps because my leaving had been so completely unpre-
pared for and the separations so multi-faceted, violent and
numerous. Perhaps I had never really progressed to the final
stage of bereavement – that of picking up life again, forming
new relationships and moving on. Yes, I had done so in the
UK of course, and my life for the past few years had been
pretty much on an even keel. But for a long time there had
been a part of me that had not been sure where I really
belonged and at times I had felt a strong pull to come back
and live in Rwanda one day. It seemed that being back in
'my' house had begun to enable me to separate the past from
the present and realise where my real home was. In a strange
kind of way that was exciting for me. It meant I could view
Rwanda through the eyes of a visitor. I would be able to
come and go, enjoying being in the country and spending
time with friends, but without the constant questioning and
anxiety in the back of my mind as to whether I would ever be
able to live here permanently and make it home again. No,
my home was back in Britain: in my little house and garden
in Ware, and among my family in Scotland and my friends
spread far and wide. The search for belonging had been
long, but at last I might be on the way to finding it.

Leaving Gahini this time did not feel so sad. Yes, there
were huge frustrations at not having had sufficient time to
spend with those dearest to me, but I knew I would come
back before too long. The month's journey through Rwanda
had been tough – and would yet be tougher still – but at least
this would be one of the helpful things I could take away at
the end of it.

11

Murambi Genocide Memorial

There was silence in the bus as we travelled. We all knew what was ahead and no one wanted to face it. I had never been to Murambi before but I had seen the images on the TV and had always had to turn away, unable to face the horror. Now I was going to see it for myself, and I was dreading it.

I stared hard out of the window as the bus bumped and lurched along from one pot-hole to the next. Suddenly the scenery all around seemed terribly interesting. So many different shades of green, the vastness of the clear blue sky offering an easy freedom and peace to the birds far above. I found myself thinking about my garden back home, looking forward to the jobs I'd have to do when I got back. Which vegetables should I plant? Will my shed have dried out enough for me to paint it? Where should I store the chopped wood for next winter's fires? Why on earth was I thinking of such things? Up until this point I hadn't given a second thought to life back in the UK but at this precise moment it seemed very important. How I longed to be back in the predictability and safety of my little house and garden in Ware. How I wished I could leave behind all this pain and trauma, to wake up in the morning and discover it had all been a terrible nightmare. If only there were *some* way of avoiding the dreadful scene I would shortly have to face.

We turned off the main earth road and onto what I could

only describe as a driveway leading up to a large half-built building a few hundred metres away. The drive was partly laid with small stones, neatly edged with an open wire fence, behind which were large expanses of newly sown grass. There was a sense of great openness and space, the surrounding hills being quite far back, and with neither houses nor fields encroaching too closely on the area.

As we approached the building, the sound of electric drills and hammering grew louder. Some twenty to thirty men were scattered around, inside and out, a few carrying building materials, a few cementing or hammering, but most seemingly just hanging around watching. I had expected the memorial site to be quiet and private, so I felt confused and disappointed by this noise and activity all around.

The minibus drew up at the front entrance – grand concrete steps leading into a large, two-storey concrete structure, as yet without either doors or glass in the windows. Among the workers I noticed a woman, so I approached her to ask which part of the building was being used as the memorial site. She said something about going to fetch someone else, and disappeared down a dusty concrete corridor then outside, leaving us standing in what was presumably to become the entrance hall, with its large horseshoe-shaped reception desk.

For some time I watched a man crouching down, watering and smoothing over a small patch of newly cemented floor, again and again and again. I thought about how I would usually have started up a conversation with him, asking about his work, or maybe his family. Chatting with complete strangers – even asking very personal questions – is perfectly normal in Rwanda. But I felt as though I'd lost my tongue.

After what seemed like ages, a tall elderly gentleman in a faded dusty suit and tie walked into the building and approached us. He introduced himself as Emmanuel and said he would show us around. He clearly was not one of the building site workers, so I wondered where he had come from. 'I was just on my way home from church,' he explained, 'when I saw your bus turning up the drive to come here, so I realised you had come to visit. I just had to go home first to pick up my bike.'

To my surprise – and relief – he led us back outside, away from the dust and clamour into the strong bright midday sun, round the side of the building and down a path towards a row of older, single-storey buildings some five hundred metres behind the new one. We walked in silence, my heart dreading what was to come. Ironically, the setting was beautiful. This had once been a school – several rows of classrooms on the side of a gentle slope, each row fronted by a balcony with four or five classrooms leading off it. The view from the balconies and all around was stunning: mile upon mile of green, fertile rolling hillsides dotted throughout with tiny homesteads surrounded by small patches of crops. Apart from the distant building site sounds there was almost nothing to be heard. Only the occasional cries of children playing across the valleys or two birds calling back and forth to each other. It would be an idyllic location – were it not for the fact that this had been the site of one of the worst massacres in the country back in 1994.

As I looked at Emmanuel in the light I noticed a huge hole in his forehead on the hairline above his left eye. It was about the diameter of a ten pence coin and maybe half an inch deep. His face looked drawn and anxious, his eyes hung with years of grief. I was reluctant to ask him to retell his story of survival, knowing the trauma of reliving events and memories. But he assured me he had told his story many times before – to numerous journalists and TV crews and other visitors passing through – and that he saw it as his job to inform the world of what had happened here in Murambi in 1994.

'When the killing started in this area we all fled to the parish, but there were far too many of us, so we were brought here to the school with a military "escort" where there was more room for us to shelter. The militia attacked us of course, but we were able to resist, because there were many more of us than of them. So they left us, and we thought they'd gone, but after a few days they came back – this time with lorries and buses full of reinforcements from Kigali. We didn't have a chance. They finished us all off – or almost all of us. There were 50,000 people in these buildings. Only four of us survived.'

My head was swimming. It wasn't fear, anger, indignation or pain – although all of these emotions had been and would again be my response at other times. No, this time it was… emptiness, numbness, nothingness. There are times when human emotions seem to shut down completely because to feel any response – even remotely in proportion to the events being described – would be far too overwhelming to cope with. The image of 50,000 men, women and children huddled together in these buildings, being brutally, mercilessly and systematically slaughtered was way beyond my imagining. But no, it was true. Standing before me was an eyewitness. How could *anyone* have survived such a massacre?

'I was shot in the head,' Emmanuel continued, pointing to the hole in his forehead. 'I fell under other corpses and I lay there until nightfall when they left. I managed to crawl out in the dark and hid around for the next few days.'

I searched Emmanuel's face, looking for some response from him. But I saw very little. Sure, he could talk about it. He told us he had done so to many visitors before. Repeating the facts was not a problem – as long as they remained just that. Pure facts. But can the human spirit ever recover from the trauma of such experiences? Visitors to Rwanda often speak of the warmth and friendliness they find among the people there. And it's true. But so often the smiles belie the scarcely hidden anguish and torment of unspeakable memories shared by so many throughout the country.

Emmanuel pointed to a wooded area on a nearby hill. 'I hid up there in among the trees, so from there I could watch what was happening here. I saw a bulldozer come in and dig out a massive grave and shovel the bodies in. They had to put extra soil on top because there were still limbs and bits of clothing sticking above the surface. Then when the French came they planted grass over it and put up a volleyball net.' He spat out these last words with utter contempt. 'This was in the Zone Turquoise you remember.[14] It was like dying again and again.'

Eventually, Emmanuel told us, he managed to get to safety in Burundi and found treatment for his wound. But he returned to Rwanda as soon as the genocide ended in July 1994.

'When I came back here I found people were denying the massacre. They said it had never happened! So I went to the RPF and I took them to show them the sites of the mass graves. It was me who showed them what had happened, and I personally helped to unearth the bodies here. We put them all into these school classrooms and then later reburied them properly over there,' he said pointing to a concrete structure with a fence around it, near to the new building.

Later, when I was able to string some words together to ask a question, I asked him why he still stayed here. Why choose to stay in a place of death, surrounded by those who had probably played a part in the massacre? Why? Because here he was close to his murdered wife and children. Because he had no other family to go to. Because every single member of his extended family had been killed. Where else would he go?

Emmanuel unlocked the rusty red metal door of the first classroom, pushed it open and stepped back to allow us in. The smell was overwhelming. The bodies had all been preserved in lime – preserving the flesh and bones but also preserving the putrid stench of death, which bites at the back of your nostrils and fills your lungs with rotting decay. I heard someone outside retching. Rough wooden tables around the edge of this small classroom were covered with corpses. Each lay in a contorted position. One with an arm over her face as if to protect herself from the final fatal blow. Another with a hand on her rosary beads around her neck. Another with part of his skull missing. Several with broken bones and cracked skulls. There they lay, some with rags of lime-coated clothing around them, others with nothing at all to provide even the last scrap of dignity. Dignity? *Dignity*? Such a concept was utterly denied on that dreadful day here ten years before. Morality, normality – even basic humanity, everything completely turned on its head.

Even as I write this, several months on, I just cannot find words to describe that scene. I fell to my knees. I wept. I felt sick. I cried out to God. I clung to Sue. The horror was, and is, inexpressible. We looked in two more rooms – one of which contained only children. In my imagination I saw the scene in these classrooms ten years before and I thought of how it would have been if Sue's kids had been there.

That was too much. I had seen enough. There were another three rows, each row with four or five classrooms, each one had been filled with bodies. There were other rooms with ropes strung across, bearing the remains of the clothes found in the graves – clothes stripped from the bodies after the massacre but considered not worth looting. But I couldn't take any more. I stood for some time leaning on the balcony banister, breathing in the fresh air, and trying somehow to compose myself before heading off back to the waiting minibus.

We passed by one of the original grave sites – a massive great hole, although now somewhat overgrown with grass and shrubs, and surrounded by a protective fence. This too would be part of the memorial site when finished.

Back at the bus Sue and I had a rare few minutes of quiet to ourselves as the film crew returned to take more footage at the classrooms. It was then that I became aware of how terrible this experience must have been for Bosco, our translator. He was a great lad, travelling everywhere with us and joining in like part of the family. Bosco was only a young teenager when the genocide happened, and he lost his whole family – all except one younger brother, for whom he has taken great responsibility. There were many times when I found it hard to be the centre of our investigations, focussing on *my* husband, *my* loss, *my* struggles, but always conscious that Bosco's loss was in many ways much greater. And certainly his ongoing daily struggle was immensely harder than mine. But he always kept graciously in the background and talked very little about his own situation. This time, however, I was acutely aware of the trauma we shared together. He was standing alone on the steps outside the new building, head down, shoulders drooped. I walked up to him, and without a word we fell onto each other's necks, arms wrapped tightly around, tears flowing down through agonising sobs. For several minutes we stood there, clinging to each other. There was nothing to be said. Sometimes there just are no words.

After a while we talked – about God, about good and evil, about doubts and questions. The contrast between our two situations struck me forcibly. Here in Rwanda there is a huge sense of solidarity with those who have shared very similar experiences. The events of the genocide were beyond belief – but people understand that here. They don't need any explanation. Here the suffering is shared by nearly all – so to suffer great loss is normal. Bosco had no trouble finding those who understood him. But in talking with others he would always be wary of saying too much, knowing that they too had suffered much. He would have to be guarded, not offloading too much in case he added to their distress. Was there anyone at all who could be there for *him*, who could listen without bringing in their own story, who could be a parent, older sibling, friend – just there for him? And how many other 'Boscos' were there in this country? Children who had seen and experienced things no human being should ever have to face, youngsters who have had huge responsibilities thrust onto their shoulders, getting on with life and struggling for survival, caring for little brothers and sisters because there's no one else to struggle for them?

For me, in the UK, it was different. I had the loneliness of bearing a trauma and grief that very, very few could even begin to understand. But I did have people who tried to help me to carry that trauma. They may not have understood or experienced it, but when I really needed help they were there to support me and listen, without unloading their own issues onto me. For me such support was invaluable. I longed to be able to offer that support to Bosco – and the thousands of others like him – but I was not in a position to do so. I could only, like others here, share in solidarity with his grief.

The crew came back. We thanked Emmanuel – although what meaning can words have in such pain and hopelessness. I wished I could have brought some message of comfort and hope from God but I had need of it in my own life too. I thought of Job's friends and wondered if just sitting on the ground in sackcloth and ashes with Emmanuel might have been more meaningful.

We headed back to Butare. At times like this I desperately needed to be on my own. This is when I'd most like to lose myself in the Scottish hills, walking for miles and miles with a dog, just having space, silence and aloneness to take in what had just happened. Instead I had to content myself with staying in at our guest-house while the others went off into town for some food. I would be miserable company for them anyway, and no doubt they would find it easier to switch off and unwind without me there. There were some leftover samosas, peanuts and bananas to nibble – although I didn't feel in the slightest bit hungry. I just wanted to sit on my own in silence. Being alone, however, is a concept most Rwandans can't get their heads around. Alodiya (the young woman who cooked breakfasts and suppers for us) realised I had been left on my own and came through from the kitchen to chat. She listened to my very brief resume of the day, and then told me her own story. She had lost both her parents during the war, but was now recently married with a young child. She had her future ahead of her and was cheerful and optimistic. I asked if she had ever considered trying to find out what happened to her parents, but she said there was no point. She knew she would never get to the bottom of it because, as she said, 'many Rwandans are such liars.'

Perhaps I should take a lesson from Alodiya. With only a couple of days to go I was really wondering if I would ever find out more than this. I'd done what I could, but I found myself increasingly identifying with those who said 'what's the point?' The whole investigation process was so harrowing and exhausting. It seemed to be reawakening so much of my grief, but as yet had produced very little to bring even a grain of truth or comfort. But there was still one hope, perhaps. We had names of prisoners who had confessed and we had been given permission to interview them the next day. And I had new information with which to challenge Kabalira. Surely he couldn't deny his involvement when there was so much evidence against him. Maybe, just maybe, I would get to the bottom of this yet.

But tomorrow was going to be another gruelling day.

12

Butare Prison

I guess this day will always rank quite high on the 'most-horrible-days-of-my-life' stakes – and I've had a few horrible days to choose from.

We had arranged to spend the morning in Butare Prison interviewing two prisoners who, so we had been told, had confessed to their crimes during the genocide. And then in the afternoon it was to be my last opportunity to interview Pastor Kabalira, this time in prison, and confront him with the new evidence we had gained over the past few weeks.

I was feeling extremely nervous. I hate confrontation, am no good at thinking quickly on my feet – not even in English, let alone in French or Kinyarwandan – and I had never set foot inside a prison before anywhere in the world. After so many frustrations, disappointments and blind alleys over the past three weeks in Rwanda it seemed to me that a great deal hung on this day and on the information we might, or might not, extract from these prisoners. Not that the two we were due to see in the morning were suspects in my investigations. They were simply two names given to us by the Vice-Attorney as examples of prisoners who had confessed and who might be willing to tell their story to us. As it happened, one had been a member of the military, and given that Charles had been taken from the guest-house by a soldier it was just possible that this man might have some information for us. The other was a former employee of the diocese, so could perhaps have been witness to events there.

As we set off in the clapped-out faded blue Peugeot on the muddy roads after a night of heavy rainfall, I wondered for a moment if we would make it at all. Just negotiating the slight hill on the short but treacherously slippery drive from the house to the road the car was skidding wildly, almost into the hedge and ditch. I clung onto the front seat as Sue and I were flung from side to side. But the driver was completely unphased by the conditions, no doubt used to much worse, and skilfully persevered through the mud and ruts until we reached the tarmac road a few hundred metres away.

The prison was on the edge of town, far from the tarmac main road. Even before the building came into sight we knew we were approaching it because of all the pink lining the roadside. Prisoners in the public eye out on community service have to wear shorts and shirts of unmistakable baby pink. These groups of men, some with hoes slung over their shoulders and others carrying cabbages, seemed to be heading back to prison after working in a field somewhere. They were accompanied by a number of armed guards and the sight might have been comical were it not so intimidating.

Through the wrought iron bars of a tall double gate we could see into a kind of courtyard area, almost like a small street with dusty beige, one-storey brick buildings on either side. At the far end was another very high brick wall with a solid metal gate – the inner chambers, well protected from the public view.

The prisoners were filing one by one through a smaller, pedestrian gate into the outer yard, leaving behind their tools before entering and being carefully frisked as they stepped inside. We climbed out of the car and headed for a small gatehouse where a couple of guards were leaning against a wall, watching us.

We had come to interview two prisoners, I explained. It

had been arranged by the Attorney a few days before.

'Are you lawyers?' one of them asked, suspiciously eyeing up the camera and equipment bags the others were carrying. I laughed, assuring him we were not – although many a time throughout the day I certainly wished I had had a lawyer's skills. The guards pointed us in the direction of the director's office half way down the row of brick buildings in the outer section. It was still quite early in the morning but already it felt stiflingly hot inside the reception. I preferred to wait outside, from where I could also get a better look at the situation around me.

After some discussion it was decided to allocate to us a small room opposite, very dark and dingy. There was a large wooden table in the middle with a hole in it, a couple of rickety wooden chairs, a few sacks of potatoes in the corner and a shelf unit with piles of yellowing, insect-eaten papers stacked in it. Everything was covered in a thick layer of creamy-brown dust. Preparing the room took some time. Cameras from two angles, a light supply with trailing extension to a neighbouring room with the nearest power socket, a few extra chairs brought in, all five of us plus Richard the photographer who had joined us for the final week. We were falling over each other. We propped the door open – the doorway providing the only source of natural light – although with other prisoners passing by or sitting on the low wall just outside, our privacy was somewhat compromised.

Our first interviewee arrived and at last we were ready to invite him in. On one side of the table Sue sat beside me so I could translate for her. Opposite us sat Boneface. I began by introducing us both and explaining what we were doing in Rwanda. I told him I had requested the interview, not because I suspected him of involvement in Charles' murder, but because I had been told he had confessed to his own crimes. After several disturbing weeks of hearing confusing and conflicting truths, half-truths and lies, I still had a little hope that it might help to hear from someone who had been in the area at the time, and who was prepared to tell the truth. Even as I said that, though, I knew I had little hope. 'Someone who was prepared to tell the truth.' What did that mean? Surely everyone we had met so far had insisted that they were telling the truth. Whose truth really is the truth? At the end of the day, what *is* truth? I felt I no longer knew.

Boneface nodded in appropriate places, listening intently and watching me closely but his face remained stonily expressionless. Were these people from the television, he asked, pointing his chin briefly in the direction of Jay and Ray. I explained about the documentary, that its focus was not at all on him but on my journey in search of my late husband's murderers. He might not even appear in it at all, but if he was in any way concerned or reluctant then his voice and his face could be altered in the final version to preserve his anonymity. He gave a kind of sneer. Why should that bother him, he said. After all, he had been to the International Tribunal in Arusha to give evidence and had been interviewed by several TV and radio stations. He was prepared to speak out and tell the truth. 'But where has that got me?' he asked, disparagingly. 'I'm still here, locked up in this prison.' I asked if he knew why he was locked up, and if he would be prepared to tell us.

'Crimes of genocide,' he replied immediately. 'That's all they would tell me. I was arrested in 2001.' I was struggling. As someone who likes – totally unrealistically – to establish some kind of rapport and warmth with a person within the first few seconds of any conversation I was finding it extremely hard to be getting only cold stares and short answers in response. Inwardly, of course, I reminded myself that I could expect nothing else in this context. A prisoner suspected of crimes of genocide is hardly likely to warm to a foreign woman surrounded by cameras asking questions about his crimes. But this was a completely new context for me and it was a huge challenge to know how best to handle it. I was trying hard to combine firmness, clarity and gentleness without betraying my deep inner angst, but it was not easy.

Boneface told us he had left the army in the early 1990s so he would probably not be able to help us much. But at my request he agreed to tell us his own story.

He had been staying locally with an army captain while working in a nearby factory, 'for matches,' he repeated in English, seeing some slight hesitation on my face. 'Ah, so you speak English,' I said, smiling, still in Kinyarwandan. 'Shall we speak in English then? That would be much easier – save me having to translate!' He smiled back and shook his head. 'I only speak a little.' But it was enough to have broken the ice and establish a little bit of that rapport I was searching for. And it was enough to serve as a warning to us to be careful of any off-the-cuff comments in English.

Boneface continued. In April 1994 when the President's plane was shot down he had been aware of killings starting in Kigali and elsewhere, but in Butare things were quiet. Two weeks later, on 20 April, the new President had come to Butare. Apparently he told people that they were being disrespectful to him and not doing as he had asked them. On the night of the 20–21 April a plane arrived from Kigali full of soldiers who set up and manned roadblocks all over the area. 'That night we heard shooting everywhere.'

Boneface described how he had been forced to kill a young Tutsi girl who had sought refuge in the house where he was staying. Initially he had pleaded for the girl's life and refused to carry out the orders, but after being threatened with his own life and that of his Tutsi girlfriend if he refused he eventually carried out the murder. He described the long, drawn-out process in some detail, remembering how he had tried only to wound her, not kill her, but she had then been left bleeding outside until the next day when he was compelled to finish her off with a kitchen knife because the house owner did not want the sound of guns in his garden.

I remembered Tutsis back in 1994 describing how they were 'hunted down like wild animals' and it struck me that even our treatment of animals is infinitely more humane than these sickeningly barbaric atrocities committed against human beings. Did human life have absolutely no value whatsoever?

Boneface continued. He spoke of a number of local high-ranking army officials who would meet regularly in the captain's house. Not being familiar with military ranking and confused by the various names, I began to write them down. One was now in exile in the UK, another had fled to Congo, another had been killed, and another was here in the prison. He had no doubt that all had been heavily involved, having heard for himself the discussions between them in the house in the evenings. He even described the areas of Butare in which each of these senior-ranking men were responsible for organising the killings. 'The one who was leading the group in the area of the diocese was a second lieutenant by the name of Gatsinzi Modeste,' he told us. 'He's here in this prison.'

This was major news. If this Gatsinzi was responsible for the area in which the diocese was situated then undoubtedly he would have known the driver of the car in which Charles was abducted – perhaps even ordered it or driven it himself. I double-checked that he was referring to the diocese of the Episcopal Church and not that of the Catholic Church. 'It was Gatsinzi who was in charge,' he confirmed 'according to the reports I was hearing from the others.'

'So he might have been the one who was driving the car?' I asked. 'I was told it was a senior ranking officer with stripes on his shoulder.' He shook his head. 'I don't think Gatsinzi drives,' he said. 'But whatever, as the one in charge of the area, no other senior person would have driven to arrest someone without his knowing about it.'

'So if he's in prison here, do you see him sometimes? Has he confessed to anything?'

'He's in for life,' he responded immediately. 'He's been questioned. He might have confessed to something, I really don't know. I can't implicate him because I didn't see anything myself. I'm only going by what I was hearing in the house.'

I asked again about who might have actually driven the car. Looking at the list I had written of senior ranking officials he pointed out very few who actually drove their own cars. The most likely one had already fled to Congo. Clearly this second lieutenant Gatsinzi Modeste was the one we should try to interview if at all possible. We might have some time in the afternoon, but realistically it was highly unlikely that we would be given permission at such short notice. Meanwhile I wanted to find out what he knew of Pastor Kabalira.

'Kabalira is here in this prison. Personally I don't really know him,' he admitted. 'He was here already before I came.' So what had he heard said about him and his involvement with the militia? 'I can tell you, from what I hear in prison no one here implicates him at all. Of the people who were working in that area around the diocese there is not one who speaks of him.' This came as a great surprise. 'What you say is very different indeed from what people outside are saying.'

'But you have to understand why people outside are implicating others,' he responded immediately, leaning forward and gesticulating more with his hands. His animation also meant he began speaking faster and I struggled even more to follow what he was trying to tell me. 'There are two reasons,' he repeated. 'Those who are outside assume that anyone locked up must be guilty and so they automatically blame them. They think anyone inside is a murderer. Also, they don't want to accept what they themselves have done and be implicated, so they put the blame onto someone else.' The first I could accept. But the second? Surely these people were being hunted down themselves! What on earth would they be blamed for?

'Yes, that's exactly it!' he replied. 'How many actually saw what was going on? Maybe one or two in every hundred? The killing was happening in broad daylight. What Tutsi is going to stand at the side of the road watching, saying so-and-so was killed by so-and-so? They were hiding; they were under beds, above the ceiling, in the undergrowth. They couldn't see! So how can they testify?"

My mind flashed rapidly back over the testimonies we had heard against Kabalira. Doroteya banging the arm of the chair in tears: 'Kabalira took my family. He went with them and they were killed.' The lady cleaning by the cathedral insisting: 'I saw him going with the militia, wearing his dog-collar and carrying a weapon.' Archdeacon Zakariya from his bed telling us he saw him with a gun. Esther, the prison guard who sees him regularly in prison saying, 'I tell him, "I know what you have done." He cannot deny it.' Were they all wrong? Were they all making it up, trying to protect them-selves, assuming Kabalira's guilt? It was possible, but seemed most unlikely.

Just at that moment we were interrupted by a man hovering at the doorway of our little room. Could I please come and answer a couple of questions with someone from the social services? How bizarre! But we had also had more than our allocated time with Boneface and still had one other person to see before lunch. The interview came to an abrupt end.

The next interviewee was of no help. He had been the chauffeur for the Bishop and as such had been around the diocesan compound during the day but latterly had been told not to come to work. He insisted he was not aware of who was in the guest-house, nor had he seen anything untoward. He was trying slimily hard to please us, while at the same time having absolutely nothing helpful to say. It took quite some time even to get these little bits of information from him because he seemed to delight in going into much irrelevant detail. I had to listen intently throughout, never knowing if there might be some small gem of useful information in the midst of the dross. Already irritated by his manner, I nearly lost it when, as he was about to leave at the end of the interview, he gave me another forced smile and asked if I would give him some money.

It's true that prisoners have a dreadful lot, and if this man's family were extremely poor or lived far from the town so could not easily come to see him and bring food, then he would be surviving on very, very little. No doubt he saw us as rich Westerners who represented a rare opportunity. But his attempts to ingratiate himself with us had been far from subtle, and this final request I found particularly tasteless, given the nature of our visit. I was hot and tired. We had been cooped up in this tiny room all morning, and my brain was throbbing with the effort of concentrating on intense and disturbing conversations in my third language. I guess we were all desperate for a break.

We dropped in to the Attorney's office on the way back to our house and to our great surprise he was there. Then to our even greater surprise he immediately agreed to an interview in prison with the second lieutenant, whom Boneface had told us about – and that the interview could take place that afternoon. There had been many frustrations and setbacks during our weeks in Rwanda, but unhelpful, bribe-seeking authorities had certainly *not* been one of them.

Over lunch I tried to think how best to phrase my questions to Gatsinzi in the afternoon. I was not thinking coolly or logically at all. Whether it was exhaustion, anxiety, stress or simply a total lack of experience in this whole business, I was struggling. Jay seemed particularly good at suggesting helpful, leading questions and I dearly wished it could be her leading the interview and not me. On many occasions over the past weeks I had felt a bit pathetic, but at this moment I was feeling more useless than ever. I'm sure most people would find the adrenaline rushing at this point – here we were, having just discovered crucial information that could well lead to a breakthrough in our search, on the verge of the most significant interviews of our whole visit – but I was dreading it.

As I had done in the morning, I spoke in Kinyarwandan to Gatsinzi, inviting him into the room and to join us at the table. However, he stood at the door and looked indignantly at the film crew. He spoke in French.

'What are these people doing?' he asked defiantly, but with a forced smile on his lips. 'Why are they filming me?' Taken aback by his questions, although legitimate, and keeping my cool I suggested he might like to sit down so I could explain my purpose – our purpose – here in Rwanda and in particular in the prison.

'We are here to...' I began, but he interrupted me abruptly. 'I was not asked if I would give my permission to be filmed,' he said with slow, calculated deliberation, staring first at me then looking round at the others in the room. 'You have no right to film without asking me first.'

'We have permission from the Ministry,' I responded, switching to French, and wondering if a prisoner had the right to refuse when the authorities had granted permission. I briefly explained our purpose here in Rwanda. He listened carefully without any further interruption. 'So their interest is in following *my* story, and you are just one of many whom we have met and interviewed,' I concluded. 'Is this clear?'

He looked slowly around the room, the peculiar smile returning to his lips. 'And who are these other people?'

'This is my sister, who is accompanying me,' I explained, 'and the other four are directors and photographers for the documentary.' He pointed his chin in the direction of Jay, then looked back at me. 'And the woman there?' he asked. Jay was attached to a camera. It was surely pretty obvious that she was part of the team. Was that so very odd?

'She's one of the directors of the documentary,' I replied, noticing his unsuccessful attempt to stifle a sneering grin. Gatsinzi was obviously not used to seeing women in the media. He was doing himself no favours. His manner was quite menacing, but also highly suspicious, as though he had something to hide. I certainly felt intimidated, but I was determined not to let him get the upper hand in any way whatsoever. Presumably he was insisting on speaking French to try and prove that he was an educated man and perhaps he found it demeaning that I should speak to him in Kinyarwandan – although this had not been a problem for anyone else up until now.

I translated the gist of the conversation thus far, and suggested to the team that it might be helpful to show our official documents at this point. During the pause while they unearthed the papers I asked Gatsinzi, 'Would you prefer to conduct the interview in English, French or Kinyarwandan? It's all the same to me.' My motive was not entirely an altruistic one or out of respect for him. I was probably thinking subconsciously, 'If you can play the education game, then so can I, mate. You won't get one up on me in that area.' Right from the beginning here I felt my metaphorical fists were clenched ready for a boxing match. This was to be a totally different experience from the morning's interviews.

His choice of French was actually an advantage for me. Not only was I more comfortable speaking French, but I also assumed (though wrongly, as it turned out) that the others would pick up most of what we were saying so there would be less need for me to translate as we went along. The official ministerial papers seemed to provide sufficient evidence that we were not about to give in to his protestations, and after scrutinising them for a few seconds he handed them back without further comment. I explained the facts, as far as I knew them, leading up to the abduction of Charles from the guest-house. 'And as you were responsible for the area around the diocese,' I went on, 'I presume you would know who it was who drove the car in which Charles was taken – if it wasn't you yourself.' At that point his grin returned, he raised his eyebrows and he looked away. 'I understand,' was all he said. 'What was the name of your husband?' he asked.

'Bilinda – Charles,' I replied, at which point he immediately looked away and I noticed the grin suddenly disappear. 'Bilinda – Charles,' he repeated thoughtfully. I was pretty sure he knew who I was talking about, but he was a master at the art of playing cool. Where was he from? When did he come? How did he get here? When did he disappear? I answered as much as I knew, all the time wondering if I should hold back any information. Was I giving too much away, making it easier for him to fabricate a denial and create an alternative story, should he need to? I was completely clueless about how to handle this interview. He weighed up the facts I had told him. 'Unfortunately I don't know him,' he responded calmly, smiling at me. 'I don't even know the car you are talking about.'

Contrary to the information our first interviewee had given us, Gatsinzi told us that his area of responsibility was the army training camp in the town, and that he had nothing to do with the area around the diocese. He did occasionally work outside of the camp, he said, but only when called upon to restore order, for example to stop looting of vacant property. So had Boneface got it wrong? He had specifically mentioned Gatsinzi as the one responsible for the area around the diocese and he had made no mention of an army training camp. At the beginning of my conversation with Gatsinzi I had stated that I knew it was him who was responsible for that area, and he had not denied it. Was he now conveniently inventing for himself an alternative story to render the rest of our questioning futile? I had no way of verifying it. We carried on. He gave me the names of the captain and colonel[15] from whom he took orders, and told us there were around ten senior ranking men in the Butare area. He was specific in his detail of the number of soldiers guarding the diocese – 'one sergeant and three soldiers' – and yet he was unable to name the person responsible for the area around the diocese, the position that according to Boneface was held by Gatsinzi himself.

I felt as though I was constantly coming up against a brick wall. He repeatedly claimed that he had been in the camp so was not aware of what was happening outside. He insisted that there were so many refugees passing through the town that it would be impossible to track down one individual, and that he knew nothing of anyone who might have been sent to the diocese to collect Charles. All this despite the fact that the person who had collected Charles had been a soldier of senior rank – of whom there were only around ten in the area – and that Charles had been taken from the very area which Gatsinzi was said to have controlled.

I was growing increasingly convinced that this was a cover-up. But I was also growing intensely frustrated at the impossibility of the situation and my inability to pin him down at all. And of course, as always, there was a nagging doubt in my mind that he might be telling the truth – unlikely, but nevertheless possible. I tried a desperate measure.

'What do you have to lose if you admit that it was you, or that you know the person who took him?' It was a stupid question, really. What would he have to lose? He would have everything to lose. He had already woven together a version of events, whether true or false, and to change that in any way now would immediately show his story to be inconsistent, potentially opening the floodgates. No, he was not likely to give anything away now. But I persevered.

'Where did you take the people who were to be killed?' I asked. 'I think it may have been you who took my husband. I would like to know where you put him.' Predictably this brought not only an outright denial but also a vehement declaration of innocence. 'We have been locked up here for nothing,' he told me angrily. 'I have killed no one. I am not a criminal. If you don't believe me, time will tell. In a short time from now I will be out of here,' he added menacingly, 'and you will know that I am innocent.'

'Yes,' he said, responding to my offer to come back and apologise if I was shown to have wrongly accused him. 'Yes, you will come back, and I will forgive you.' He had changed now from the formal *vous* to the more informal, or in this case condescending, *tu* form. 'But if you don't come back,' he continued, staring me straight in the face, the sides of his mouth and his nostrils twitching in what I took to be barely controlled anger, 'you must know that your heart will condemn you for this terrible accusatory behaviour.'

I had tried questions, I had shown him photographs, I had tried persuading, and now even gone as far as accusing, but nothing had taken me any further towards knowing the truth. I had come to the end of my resources. A guard appeared in the doorway, reminding us that the prison would shortly be closing to visitors. If we wanted to spend the few final minutes with Kabalira then I would have to bring the interview with Gatsinzi to a close.

I had been unaware of Kabalira's presence outside at the time, but reviewing the video tapes later it was clear that much of the time he had been standing with his back to us, right outside the doorway, presumably overhearing most of our conversation. Also obvious on the videotapes, as we talked in English among ourselves and for a few moments ignored Gatsinzi, was that he could clearly be seen looking out of the doorway and gently shaking his head. A message to Kabalira? Meaning?

We had only a few minutes with Kabalira, but it was our last chance. Since the first meeting with him we had gathered a number of testimonies from people who claimed he had been directly involved with the militia. Would he confess, when faced with this new evidence? Not surprisingly, I suppose, he denied it all flatly. He constantly insisted that if there was anything else he could say to help me, he would be only too willing to do so but as a pastor he could only tell the truth. He did admit having seen the driver of the car that took Charles away, but it had only been a brief glimpse of someone he did not know, and it had happened ten years ago so he would not be able to identify him now. Basically, it was much the same as the first interview. Despite all our efforts and heartache over the past three and a half weeks, it felt as though we had made no progress whatsoever. A guard had been hovering at the door for some time, reluctantly interrupting us twice now to ask us to finish. It was well past four o'clock and we had been stuck in that tiny room since morning. I was not sorry to go. And I hoped fervently that I would never have to go back there again.

By the time we reached our house I felt near breaking point. I was utterly, utterly wrung out – physically, mentally and emotionally. It had been a huge mental effort to spend a whole day speaking and listening in two other languages and trying to translate all the way through – especially when it was essential that I understand fully what was being said. I could not be content just to catch the general gist. The content of what we had been hearing was at times extremely disturbing – detailed accounts of gruesome murders evoking acute memories in me of the events in 1994. It had taken all my wisdom and more to try and find ways – usually unsuccessfully – of phrasing questions in such a way as to elicit the truth and get to the bottom of what actually happened to Charles. On top of all that was the unbearable frustration that Gatsinzi and Kabalira clearly knew much more than they were prepared to say, yet I was completely powerless to force them to speak. I felt as if I had been abused. To retell my story and ask for their help had made me extremely vulnerable and I felt as though they had taken pleasure in stamping all over my fragility with their size twelve hobnailed boots. Gatsinzi's lewd smile throughout much of the interview had said it all.

Three and a half weeks of travelling, searching, questioning – desperate to find answers. And what had I gained? Nothing. Only distress, confusion and pain. And now, to cap it all, I was afraid. I had accused someone of complicity in a crime without any concrete proof. It had clearly angered him and his response was intensely threatening. 'In a short time from now I will be free and *you will know* that I am innocent,' he had repeated menacingly a few times.

Was I in the wrong to have accused him? Might my own life be threatened? I might be going home to the relative safety of the UK, but who was to say that this influential man would not have his contacts around the world? I might be put on a hit list. This might seem a bit far-fetched to anyone reading now, but at the time it was real for me and I was very afraid. I have since learned that legally I would have nothing to worry about – but what respect does any possible mass murderer have for the rule of law? If I had had any further question as to why more people in Rwanda do not try to find out the truth about their murdered relatives, it was now gone. This was a question I had asked myself many a time in the lead up to, and the early days of our trip. But now I knew. It was probably not so much the more obvious financial question – of the time, energy and travel costs involved in investigating – though that in itself would deter most people. Nor even the awful trauma of bringing back to mind and reliving the atrocities of 1994. No. It was – as many people have since told me – the humiliation, the distress, the horror of facing those probably responsible for the deaths of our loved ones, only to have them stare us straight in the face and deny all knowledge. And on top of that to live then with the fear that the questioning and challenging might put one's own life at risk. I think I now begin to understand part of the reason why rape victims are often so reluctant to take their attackers to court. It is like experiencing the abuse all over again and being totally powerless to change anything.

I had begun this journey with the challenge of finding and forgiving those responsible for Charles' death. But gradually I had realised it was not so simple. Charles did not die because of one person's actions but as the result of a long chain of events. I had now met two people who could well have been significant links in that chain, and whose actions may have had a direct bearing on his death. Were these the people to whom I had hoped to offer forgiveness? To say that I was struggling with forgiveness at this point would be absolute rubbish. The concept did not even enter my head! All I knew was that my mind and emotions were in total chaos. As we stood together on the patio outside our house, debriefing the day's events without even going inside, the whole trembling jumble inside me welled up and spilled out in a flood of tears and sobs.

The crew, Sue and Bosco were fantastic. They listened, they affirmed me, they assured me I had said nothing harmful and we even ended up laughing over some little incidents earlier on in the day. Suddenly, as I began to calm down again, I realised I was extremely hungry. The emotions of the day had used up all my energy reserves and I was desperate for something sweet. Jay and Phil popped into town to try and find some chocolate and came back with a few bars of dodgy Kenyan Cadbury's and a bottle of hard-to-find red wine. Over supper the evening took on a feel of post-exam euphoria as we indulged in our precious treats, laughing over silly jokes and playing cards.

I felt as if the day had turned me into an elastic band, stretched almost to breaking point, and then suddenly let loose to relax and unwind. The trip was almost over and whatever the final day threw at me I knew it could never be worse than today had been.

Next day was our last full day in Rwanda and the crew wanted to take me back to the guest-house, to the room in which Charles had spent his last days alive. I was not particularly enthusiastic about the idea, remembering my painful visit there when back in the country in October 1994. But since that time, a lot of water had gone under the bridge and I wondered if I might see things differently now.

The guest-house was extremely sparse. A few steps led to the entrance, then a short passageway split off at right angles into a long, concrete corridor to the left and right. Dark wooden doors lined both sides but as they were all closed the only natural light came from the entrance door. It was a very dismal place indeed. I walked along the corridor, checking the numbers on each door. 'Thirteen, eleven. Ah, here it is. Number Nine.' I guess it had been the Bishop who had told me on my first visit the number of the room in which Charles had been. Certainly the number nine had stuck with me. The wobbly door handle almost came off in my hand, and the door opened less than halfway before bumping onto the metal frame of the bed. Other than two beds, one on either side wall (with less than a bed's width between them) the only 'furniture' was a block of wood screwed to one wall with no hooks attached and a single light switch. The walls had been painted bright green and the floor was dull grey concrete.

I had forgotten how tiny and bleak these rooms were. It was awful to think of Charles spending his last days in such a place – but I suppose if there was one thing I had learned on this trip it was that he had not been alone. The kindness and hospitality of Jeannette and Philippe nearby would surely have been of some comfort to him in his fear and loneliness.

I sat on the edge of the bed and looked around. It felt strange to be here on our last day in Rwanda, and to think that this had been the place where Charles had spent his last days. But I was about to fly back home to safety and peace whereas he had been about to go to his death. I felt a strong sense of finality, of all things coming to an end. Yet still, after all the searching and heartache, I was no nearer to finding out exactly what had happened to him. Or was I? For years I had assumed I would never know. Then in the months leading up to the trip I had begun to realise there *was* perhaps a slight possibility of finding out, if only we could find the relevant people. The past three and a half weeks in the country had seen my hopes rise and fall so many times as we followed up lead after lead. But every time the information

seemed to skirt around the edges of the details of his death
and never get right to the heart of it. People were willing to
talk – but they were not the right people.

Then just yesterday, for the first time, I realised that there
were people who knew. Yesterday, right at the end of our trip,
just a couple of days before leaving the country and ending
the search, I came face to face with a real possibility of
finding out the truth once and for all. It was there, just at the
edge of my grasp – but *I could not reach it.* I could not
persuade, plead with, insist on or cajole Gatsinzi or Kabalira
into giving me the information I needed. I just could not do
it. And that was unbelievably frustrating. So infuriatingly
close, but not there. I realised at that moment that I would
never get to the truth – short of a miracle happening, a work
of God, perhaps, and a complete turn around in attitude to
one of contrition and repentance. I would have to go back to
my original position of living with the unknown.

The whole purpose of this trip had been to get to the truth
of what had happened to Charles at his death. I had failed in
my objective. It called into question whether there had been
any point at all in coming. And yet the trip had not been
entirely useless. One unexpected truth I had discovered had
been the extent of Charles' relationship with Martine.
Hearing this had made it clear to me that our marriage
probably – very likely – would not have worked. This had
been shattering news – yet also in a strange way liberating.
Now I could let go of the hope of what might have been.
This felt like quite a significant step in accepting the reality
of what had happened and the implications for now and the
future. It felt like another letting go of broken dreams and
shattered hopes – but in a freeing kind of way. A loosening
of the ties that had long bound me with Rwanda. A way,
which allowed me to move on in my life as it is now.

As I sat reflecting to Sue I also realised that over these
weeks I had made myself face things, which for years I had
carefully avoided. Back in the comfort of the UK I had a fair

idea of the triggers that would set me off into a downward spiral of desolation and bleakness over the memories of the events here. And I always made a point of steering well clear of them. But here I could not avoid them. Visiting the memorial site, hearing eyewitness accounts of atrocities, listening to lies and contradicting reports, being back in a climate of betrayal and confusion – these had all been in my face so much throughout our visit. It had been awful to go through the experiences, but perhaps facing them head on had now taken some of the sting out.

Several people had told me it was not a good time to be in the country. 'This is our time of mourning,' they had said. 'You should come back in the summer when the remembrance period is over. We'll be happier then.' But it was important for me to be here over this time, to share with them in the tenth anniversary commemorations, to remember our sadness and grieve together. I knew all this in theory. And I sensed that when I got home, and after the dust had settled a bit, I would see the value of this month and how it had changed me. But at that moment as I sat there on the bed in Room Nine, every corner of my being felt weary and wrung out, right to the centre of my bones.

I did not want to go. I did not want to walk out of that room knowing I would not return to it for years, if ever. It had been Charles' last place. And despite all that had happened and all I had learned, I still loved him. I wanted to hold onto the past but the past was not here. It could never be the same again and I knew I had to move on.

It took a huge effort to stand up from the bed and walk out of the door, along the corridor and back down the steps into the dazzling sunlight.

13

Coming Home?

'Just left Rwanda en route for Nairobi,' began the entry in my journal for Wednesday 21 April 2004.

Strange mixture of emotions leaving. This trip has felt quite unreal in many ways – travelling with people I don't really know, spending a lot of time in places I don't really know, living in hotels and guest-houses, jumping in and out of our own taxis. So very different from my usual experience of Rwanda. But also, it has been extremely intrusive, pushing into people's lives as well as pushing myself to go through some terribly difficult experiences after which I feel utterly wrung out. I'm very sleepy, so it's hard to tell how I'm really feeling. More numb than anything, because it'll take time to process it all – but there's sadness, relief, anticipation, sense of normality...

Sadness and regret – at not spending enough time with those I love; at leaving behind those who have huge problems without being able even to scratch the surface of them. But interestingly not really any sadness at leaving behind my life that was, because of a realisation that it isn't my life any more and I've changed. It's almost as if I look back on me then as a different person and life has moved on now. I can let go of the painful experiences as well as the fun ones and move on.

Relief – because it really was hard to put myself through all that. Relief that I'm going back to a place where I can take people at face value, where there's electricity and hot running water all the time, where I can have space in my house to myself again, and that I can get on with 'normal' life, where issues are trivial and people around me have little to worry about.

Anticipation, however, because of the new direction the CBMT might take and how we may be able to spread our support much wider. And at the prospect of keeping in more regular contact with folk through email. So much easier now that we have re-established contact. And anticipation at coming back again soon.

A sense of normality – in that I won't feel obvious and sticking out like a sore thumb wherever I go. I'm used to it in Rwanda, but there were so few bazungu in some places where we went that I felt pretty obvious. It's a novelty much of the time, but sometimes it became really wearing.

But, big progress in realising how I've moved on in terms of sense of belonging. Remember feeling so horribly rootless when I came back before in 1994 – and for years. Had the benefit of feeling at home in both cultures but disadvantage of not belonging to either. Didn't really 'fit' anywhere. Now realise there's something about being able to go, visit, enjoy, live, interact – without feeling the need to convince myself I could live back there again. I don't have to belong there at all. I can go as an outsider, visit and come back again.

The search for roots had been a long one. Not that I had had an unstable childhood – far from it. I had lived in the same house in Montrose from birth until I left school to go to university. But from then onwards I had moved house/flat/lodgings on average about once a year. I grew to love this somewhat itinerant lifestyle, facing new challenges, travelling, meeting new people. But the four and a half years I spent in Rwanda were by far the longest I had been in one place for a long time. Little wonder I had put down roots there and come to feel I belonged. I was expecting it to be my home for the rest of my life. No doubt it would have been easier had I made a decision to leave Rwanda and then spent several months preparing and working up to the separation. But that was not to be. When I left in March 1994 it was with a small holiday bag packed for the beach – and the assumption that I would be returning two weeks later. I had done absolutely nothing to prepare for leaving the country indefinitely.

Coming back to the UK in 1994 did not feel like coming home. For a start I had no home base to return to. My parents had separated only two months previously so they had enough problems of their own without me adding to them. I was not homeless, though. My manager at Tearfund, in an amazingly generous and thoughtful gesture, moved out of her London flat for as long as I wanted it, providing me with a safe place to hide for three weeks. She was close enough to be there for the support I needed, but far enough away to allow me to spend my days in shock, hidden away from most human contact, glued to the TV and radio news reports from Rwanda. But it was not home.

Over the next two years my sister Sue and her family were equally generous and flexible in juggling their rooms and their lives to allow me to stay with them, giving me a stable base and love while I gradually began to pick up the pieces. But the moving continued – into student halls of residence, rented houses, living with a friend with a disability and then finally into my own house. The novelty of change was definitely wearing off and I was beginning to long for a place to belong.

My ties with friends in Rwanda had been maintained over the years and the pull to return was strong. Each time I went back for a visit it was as if part of me had come home at last, while another part of me felt like a complete stranger there; I would return to the UK unsettled and confused.

Christian friends (far more spiritual than I am!) have reminded me that my true home is not here on earth anyway but in heaven. How true that is – and I agree with them, as a position of faith. But here on earth I suspect I may not be the only earthly mortal who still needs a place where I *feel* I belong. Over the past few years I have gradually begun to realise the complex and wide-reaching effects the genocide has had on my own life. For a long time I had been so conscious of how much greater was the grief and suffering of my friends in Rwanda that I had barely allowed myself to recognise my own pain and grief. But writing a research paper a few years ago on 'Re-entry as Bereavement', looking at expatriate workers coming back to live in their country of origin, I began to acknowledge that my own loss had been quite complicated, and how this in turn has affected my struggles over where I belong.

I had been grieving not only the loss of my husband and several good friends, but also the loss of what had been my home and my life. I had had no time to prepare for leaving, to say any goodbyes to people or places or to gear myself up psychologically for such a major transition. I had left with highly ambiguous feelings, towards Charles in particular and the culture in general, resulting from my experience of betrayal and not knowing whom I could trust. Each of these factors had added to the twisted knot of the grieving process for me and it has taken quite some untangling to separate the strands.

I remembered how important it had been for me to feel I belonged in Gahini and how much it had meant to me to be accepted as a single woman. But then I had felt very lonely during our marriage difficulties, realising how little I understood others or was understood by them, and that although I might live all my life in this country, it would never fully be home for me. I know I'm not alone in living with this tension. I share it with many from around the globe whose lives have been enriched through new experiences and the challenges of living in different countries and who have the great privilege of being at home in several places. But having lots of homes can also result in feeling we have no one true home, and for some this can be profoundly unsettling at times. This can be hardest for the single person, with no partner or children to provide continuity as they move around. Perhaps all this goes some way towards explaining why each return trip to Rwanda has filled me with such confusion and angst. And perhaps it also helps to explain why *this* time it felt so different. I had changed, moved on. Being back this time I had discovered that I could come to Rwanda, spend time with people, face the happy times as well as the painful memories but *leave* again and go back *home*, because now I recognised that I truly belong in the UK. This was a huge relief to me. However, in the early weeks of being back in the UK after our trip that initial relief was frequently overshadowed by something else.

It was touching that many people around me were interested and asking how the trip had gone, but I found it impossible even to begin to summarise it in a few sentences. I had only tasted a little of the fear, the painful memories and the uncertainty with which so many in Rwanda live, but even that would be completely beyond the experience or understanding of most people in the UK. So I had to content myself with giving them the sanitised, palatable version, and leave myself with the frustration of having no outlet for my memories.

So I began to write. It would be a way of retelling experiences I could not bring myself to talk about and I spent hours sitting by my computer reliving the previous four weeks. But then I began to sink. I went to work in the mornings, I wrote in the afternoons, and in the evenings I sat and stared into space. I didn't cry or want to talk to anyone.

I simply seemed to have lost all my energy and all I wanted was to be alone and sit in silence. I began to think that returning had been a retrograde move, a bad idea. Had it not just reopened old wounds without providing any resolution or moving forward? Was I not now much worse off than I had been before? Now, as I write this with the benefit of a year's hindsight, I realise that the four weeks back in Rwanda had taken their toll and I was first and foremost simply and utterly exhausted. But at the time I assumed that the heaviness and flatness I was feeling was a direct result of the material I was writing about and that I would have to put up with it until such time as I'd finished my writing. Fortunately, a good friend, a clinical psychologist, was able to be more objective. Debbie had spent an afternoon debriefing me a few days after my return and I think she had recognised my precarious emotional and psychological state. What I needed was some common-sense advice on looking after myself. After chatting to Debbie a few weeks later I decided to drop the writing for a time (she was right that I would be unlikely to forget the experiences for a very long time) and instead take time out having fun with people. It worked, and very gradually I found my energy returning.

So now I could function again on a more or less even keel. That was good. But not far below the surface I continued to struggle with some core issues: issues of truth, of trust and betrayal, of forgiveness and anger. What is truth? Whose truth can I trust? How is it possible to trust again when betrayal has been so deep? Is forgiveness possible or even helpful when there is so much uncertainty around? I remembered Charles' explanations of his absences from home (working late, visiting friends) and initially believing him, but later realising he was sometimes lying. I remembered the profound pain of betrayal. Then, more recently, hearing so many conflicting stories during the trip, having our hopes raised by so-called 'eyewitness accounts' but then dashed by contradictory reports from others. Even our meetings with

officials – some church leaders and government employees
– left me wondering if I'd said too much. Could I trust them?
Was their version true? Were they intentionally missing out
certain facts, or exaggerating others? Not knowing who to
believe was torment. For those with me the not-knowing
was probably more like intense frustration, but because for
me it echoed the agony of months of loneliness, helplessness
and betrayal by Charles, it was torment.

Was there perhaps some cultural element in the interpretation of truth? Coming from a western culture with a heritage
of Greek dichotomy, my understanding of truth tends to be
relatively clear cut, black and white. But to my understanding
the African concept of truth seems much more fluid and
relative. Much more important than absolute truth is the
maintenance of community and relationship. Fostering
harmony and peace – even if it means missing out or
embellishing some of the facts – would always be more
important than speaking out the full story, if that might cause
hurt or offence. I have a deep appreciation of the value of a
society based on relationship and community, concepts
largely lost in our individualistic western society. But when
it came to searching out factual information, where accuracy
and detail were all important, I felt powerless in the clash of
cultures. Western-style direct and confrontational questioning was generally completely ineffective, but I had never
mastered the art of the slowly, slowly, discreet, talking-round-
the-houses method so much more appropriate in Rwanda.
The more desperate I became to find out, the less co-
operative would be the person I was talking to. It was
infuriating – and all the more so because of the reminders of
equally desperate conversations with Charles.

But betrayal is much more profound than just a different
approach to truth. How hard it is ever to trust again when
betrayal has been so deep. Yet this is the current experience
of most Rwandans. If those with whom for years you have
lived, worked and worshipped then betray you and murder

members of your family, how do you *ever* trust anyone again? This was normality turned utterly upside down.

Ten years later and it is my impression that there is still, not surprisingly, a general undercurrent of mistrust and suspicion, and in some cases unmasked hatred. And sometimes I fear for the future of Rwanda. I remember a conversation I had in Kigali with the BBC correspondent, Fergal Keane, quizzing him on his assessment of the current situation in Rwanda. Having reported and written on Rwanda for years Fergal not only has a great insight and understanding of the country and its complexities, but also a depth of compassion for the Rwandan people. It was the tenth anniversary of the genocide and I had just done a couple of interviews with Hilary Anderson and Mike Woolridge. I mentioned to Fergal that I had made some comments I later regretted. 'Like what?' he asked me. 'Well, I said at the end something about there being a lot of anger and bitterness around, but actually that's not my experience of the people I've been meeting.' Fergal looked at me askance. 'Lesley,' he asked, 'what planet are you living on? This place is seething with anger and hatred!' I knew his work had taken him to meet hardened, embittered, violent men with no regrets about their actions in the past and determined to 'finish the job', as they would say. But all I could think of were the gracious, forgiving and generous people I'd just been spending time with. These were – and are – the two sides of the reality of Rwanda.

It is surely remarkable how stable the country has been for the past ten years. Considering how all-consuming and appalling the violence was in 1994 it is amazing that there has not been further, continuing violence, whether revenge killings or a continuation of the attempted annihilation of Tutsis and moderate Hutus.

I think of the remarkable work of people like Nicholas with his essential oil co-operatives for widows and orphans, and I'm deeply humbled. It takes only a few people filled with God's compassion, standing up for what is right and leading by example, to transform whole communities. I saw deeply traumatised women who had been all but destroyed by anger and despair but who now reach out to others with love, compassion and hope. I saw the awesome power of forgiveness in their lives – and I realised that there *is* still hope for the future of Rwanda.

Forgiveness... so simple to say; so hard to put into practice. I could see it in others' lives, but could I live it out in my own? For years I had been struggling with the concept. Could I forgive myself for my part in the failure of our marriage, or Charles for the part he had played? Could I forgive the person or people responsible for his death? And then, as well as the challenge of accepting God's forgiveness of me for my failures, I also sometimes felt I needed to forgive God for what had often seemed to me as a failure on his part to intervene and stop the genocide. But is it ever my place to forgive God? Having been a Christian for many years, I had understood, at least theoretically, the importance of knowing I was forgiven by God. But I'm not sure I had ever really grasped the enormity of its impact and implications in my life. Not, that is, until 1994.

During the first few weeks of the genocide, while I existed in a state of continuous shock, I somehow found the energy to pray desperately for Charles to be kept safe and come through alive. I used every opportunity to encourage others to do the same – but was careful not to say anything about our marriage difficulties. I was so ashamed of my failure, fearing everyone would write us off or despise us. And the last thing I wanted was for Charles to be given any blame when he was not there to defend himself. But very soon, as the situation deteriorated beyond belief and rumours began to emerge of Charles' death, I began to face the fact that I might never see him again. I would never be able to say sorry again, to receive his forgiveness, to be reconciled with him. I was taking the lion's share of the blame for our failures onto myself, and the weight of it was breaking me. It was a desperate state to be in, feeling so guilty but realising there was absolutely nothing I could do to make amends. I felt as though I would have to carry this burden of guilt forever and would never again laugh or even smile.

One particular Sunday morning Sue, Cameron and their five children had all gone off to church, but I had stayed at home alone. I just could not face people and needed some space. I remember sitting at the kitchen table, my face in my hands, feeling almost as though I had a physical weight on my shoulders preventing me from standing up straight. There was no question of stringing any words together to pray, but I sensed God was present with me. For some reason the words of some choruses I had sung in my teens came back into my mind. 'At the cross, at the cross, where my burdens fell away...' and 'Burdens are lifted at Calvary'. It must have been twenty years or more since I'd sung these songs but their words struck home to me dramatically. Then I found myself asking a question. If the central message of my faith was one of forgiveness through the death of Jesus Christ on the cross at Calvary and so through his death our 'burdens' of guilt and shame can be lifted and taken away, then why was I still bent double with my own burden? Did my Christian faith mean nothing to me now? I suddenly realised that if anyone was in need of forgiveness, it was me, now. Had there been a possibility of making amends with Charles and working things out ourselves, then perhaps forgiveness would not be so crucial. But there was *nothing* I could do now to say sorry or bring reconciliation. I was totally powerless. And that was precisely where forgiveness was the only way ahead.

It was like discovering something of the heart of God all over again – or perhaps even for the first time, because never before had I been in such a desperate state, or realised so personally the relevance of the death of Jesus. Even the physical weight I had felt hanging on my shoulders seemed to have gone. Now it's true that I was talking here about discovering God's forgiveness in my life, which would not necessarily mean that Charles had forgiven me too. But I kind of figured out that if Charles had died and was now in heaven, where there would be no more grudges or bitterness, then he'd have forgiven me too!

Of course, as soon as I began to grasp the significance of *being* forgiven, I realised there were implications in terms of my willingness or reluctance to respond by forgiving others. If *I* had been forgiven my miserable and mean thoughts, words and actions, then who was I to withhold forgiveness of others? Well I could start with Charles. I took most of the blame for our difficulties onto myself anyway, and did not consider that he had done much wrong. I still loved him very much, and it didn't feel so difficult to forgive him for the hurt he had caused me. But what of those who might have killed him? At this stage I did not know whether the rumours were true or not. Was he dead or alive? Was there anyone to forgive, and if so, would I ever know who it was? Over the years that followed, when his death had been more or less confirmed, I thought long and hard about forgiving those who had been responsible for murdering him. Was it possible to forgive someone without knowing who they were? And if I had never met them or even seen them and they were thousands of miles away, would it mean anything anyway? But I felt I had to try and forgive, for my sake if nothing else. Deep inside I was very angry and bitter over what had happened, and I knew that in time, if unchecked, this bitterness could destroy me. I had seen other twisted and angry people who had harboured their grudges and resentment over years, refusing to forgive, and they were not a pretty sight. Why should those who had destroyed our loved ones have the satisfaction of destroying us too? I felt this was as far as I could go in offering forgiveness – as long as I lived on the other side of the world and had no face to connect to the crimes. It was hard enough, but compared to the challenge of potentially meeting Charles' killers, it seemed relatively easy.

Before going to Rwanda in 2004 I had tried to imagine the different possible outcomes of our investigations. It was most likely, I figured out, that we would not be able to find anyone responsible for Charles' death. Or, if we did, they would deny it completely. I guessed it would be highly unlikely for us to find anyone who had confessed to his murder or who showed any remorse. I had not really considered that we would find people who might have been closely involved, but then be completely unable to verify or refute their testimonies because of the confusion and half-truths strewing our journey from beginning to end. What do you do when faced with someone whom you believe, but are not sure, may have had a crucial role to play in your husband's murder, but who stares you straight in the face and categorically denies it? Would forgiveness have had any meaning at all at that moment, even if I had had the guts to offer it? I'm not sure that it would. Gatsinzi was in prison for life, we had been told. As a senior military officer with great responsibilities he would not be among those eligible for release if he confessed to his crimes. Indeed, for all I knew he might be among those facing the death penalty. Having spent a couple of hours trying to convince me that he knew nothing of the circumstances around Charles' death he would probably not have been impressed by my telling him I forgave him.

I'm not saying that forgiveness means letting someone off the hook. As I see it, a personal offer of forgiveness does not absolve a person from facing a just punishment for their crimes. Justice still has to be upheld and to be seen to be done – and I don't believe national reconciliation in Rwandan will ever come about fully until that happens. But on an individual level, between perpetrator and victim, the issue is somewhat different. Forgiveness provides an opportunity for both parties to move on. Higiro was clearly moved by my tentative offer, even though I was not personally a member of Anatolie's family. He had acknowledged the crimes he had committed and had been punished for them. So it was not a case of letting him off the hook but rather, as he himself said, that when we meet again I would not continue to hold this against him. It meant he would no longer have to live with his burden of guilt and I would no longer have to live in bitterness and anger. Perhaps that sounds too simplistic. I was still, and always will be, distressed about Anatolie's death. Sometimes I don't at all *feel* like forgiving Higiro but it's a choice I have made – and continue to make. This doesn't mean to say I have forgotten. As far as I understand it, the phrase 'forgive and forget' is rubbish! How can I obliterate something from my memory? From time to time some little thing unexpectedly triggers my memories of her – her smile, her voice, an experience we shared together – and I'm plunged back into disbelief and sadness again. How easy it would be then to nurse the bitterness, but I choose not to. I choose to forgive – again, and again, and again. As long as is necessary, and as long as God gives me the guts to do so.

With Gatsinzi it is much harder. He has shown no contrition or remorse, offered no apology or even acknowledged that he has done anything wrong. And I have no proof that he is to blame, only strong hints and a gut feeling. So is it in any way appropriate to forgive? For many months after meeting him I shivered every time I thought of him or saw a picture of him. To me he was a vile, evil man. It almost felt as though I was in his grip, locked into my grief, anger and intense frustration at the helplessness I felt in the face of his blanket denials. In the last chapter I wrote of how the investigations were like facing the abuse all over again, feeling totally powerless in the presence of the perpetrator of violence who denies all responsibility. I seemed to be stuck in a no-win situation. I strongly suspected both Kabalira and Gatsinzi had had a significant part to play in Charles' death, and this sickened me. But I had no proof and I might be completely wrong, in which case I had no business offering forgiveness for something they did not do. But did it have to be this way? Would I have to live in this unbearable dilemma for the rest of my life? Or was there some way I could offer forgiveness, at least in my heart and before God though not face to face? Surely Gatsinzi's response and attitude were his own responsibility, not mine. I could do nothing about that. But I did have responsibility for my own response. It was up to me to decide whether I would let him continue to have power over me, or choose to respond differently.

It seems to me that forgiveness addresses the imbalance of power. Forgiveness says 'I am no longer in your power. You can say or do as you like, but you will not abuse me any further because I have chosen to offer you forgiveness. You may reject my offer. You may deny your actions and continue to live in hatred and anger, but that's your choice. I will not allow your choice of self-destruction to destroy me also. I am free to choose – and I choose to forgive and to live in freedom. To remain in bitterness and resentment would also destroy me.' In describing forgiveness as 'drawing out the sting in the memory that threatens to poison our entire existence',[16] Archbishop Desmond Tutu expresses my rambling thoughts much more eloquently and profoundly than I ever could. But even as I write this and continue to wrestle with the issue of forgiveness, I am conscious of the danger of falling into a 'them and us' mentality. How easy it is to write someone off because he or she is different from me. But had I had the history, the background, the ideology, of Gatsinzi or Kabalira, might I not have behaved in a similar way? How much trouble have I taken to understand the forces and beliefs that drove the extremist militia, army and government to behave in the way they did? I am in no way condoning their actions, but I need to recognise that these people are human beings too, with their own hopes and aspirations.

I recently read the testimonies of Jo Berry, the daughter

of Sir Anthony Berry MP, killed in the Brighton bomb in 1984 and of Patrick Magee, one of the IRA Brighton bombers. I was struck by her search to get into the shoes of Magee, to understand who he is as a person and what had led him to commit such an act. Her meetings and discussions with Magee over a number of years have led Jo to the realisation that 'no matter which side of the conflict you're on, had we all lived each other's lives, we could all have done what the other did. In other words, had I come from a Republican background, I could easily have made the same choices Pat made.'[17]

How easy it is to get into a blame mentality, seeing myself as completely innocent and the 'enemy' as completely evil. I would like to think that had I been in Gatsinzi's or Kabalira's shoes I would have stood up against the tide of atrocities and championed the cause of peace. But would I? Do we not share a common humanity, making me just as fallible as anyone else?

When I first went to Rwanda, life seemed so simple. There was right and wrong, good and evil, truth and lies. I was naive, I believed the best and I had high aspirations. I'm different now. Neither better nor worse, just different. Life, with all its fullness, richness and pain, has changed me. God has faithfully been by my side throughout, though at some times his presence has been more tangible than at others.

My home is not and never could be in Rwanda but many of her people continue to inspire, humble and challenge me. My relationship with that country has brought me the greatest pain and the greatest joy of my whole life. We have shared utter devastation and desolation, and for some this is still where they are. But in many others I see an amazing determination to rebuild out of the ashes, to reach out with the love of God to those around and to make music with what remains.

What an inspiration.

Notes

1 If you read the word 'Rezire' out loud it really doesn't sound too different from Lesley – especially if you remember that 'l's and 'r's are often interchanged in Kinyarwandan.

2 Pastors were usually addressed as 'Pastor', even by their wives, as a mark of respect. But to me being a pastor was Charles' role, not his whole being, so I continued to call him Charles.

3 A number of those in prison on suspicion of crimes of genocide are confessing to their crimes and pointing out the locations of mass graves. These graves are then excavated, the bones of the deceased placed in coffins, and the local community gathers to give its loved ones a dignified funeral service.

4 *Inkotanyi* or literally 'cockroaches' was the derogatory term used to describe sympathisers of the cause of the Rwandan Patriotic Front.

5 'Dollars! Bread!' With both French and English being official languages of Rwanda the kids would know that most tourists would understand one or other of their pleas.

6 The Charles Bilinda Memorial Trust (CBMT) was set up in early 1995 following the almost certain confirmation that Charles had been killed. With so many of

Rwanda's educated people having been either killed or fled the country, the need for foreign expertise was urgent. But I felt strongly that this could only be a short-term measure, and that the long-term rebuilding of the country would come from her own people. As Charles had himself had the privilege and knew the benefit of a good education, I decided that a charity in his memory should focus on supporting Rwandans through education and training opportunities, enabling them to contribute their part in the regeneration of their country. As the CBMT still continues, Nicholas and Elsie are two of many who are doing just that.

7   'Good afternoon, you hard-working people!'

8   We heard of similar situations several times – how through the day active militia would go out 'to work' as the killing was euphemistically called, but then return home at night to friends whom they were hiding in their homes.

9   When the genocide began in April 1994, Rwanda was immediately entered by the RPA – a highly motivated and disciplined force formed from Rwandan Tutsis and moderate Hutus who had fled to Uganda during uprisings against Tutsis in 1959 and later. The RPA swept rapidly south and west, halting the carnage of Tutsis and moderate Hutus as they went, and eventually took power in July 1994. Being very close to the road leading south from Uganda, Gahini was one of the first communities they passed through, and as most of the population had fled at the rumour of the RPA approach, they had their pick of the vacated property.

10 There are four levels for the *Gacaca* courts, following the administrative divisions in Rwanda – Province, District, Sector and Cell. There are also four categories of genocide crime, ranging from category 1, the organisers and instigators of the genocide, to category 4, offences against property. The ordinary Rwandan courts

have sole jurisdiction over category 1 defendants but the other three categories are investigated and tried through the *Gacaca* courts such as this one in Gahini.

11 There is now clear evidence that stockpiles of weapons were built up and distributed around the country in preparation for a mass killing of so-called *inkotanyi* – Tutsis and Rwandan Patriotic Front sympathisers. See, for example, the account of Lt Gen. Romeo Dallaire in *Shake Hands With The Devil: The Failure of Humanity in Rwanda*, Random House, Canada 2003. Dallaire was Force Commander of the UN Assistance Mission for Rwanda from 1993.

12 Under new amnesty legislation prisoners suspected of crimes of genocide who confess to their crimes are usually released from prison into the community. This has encouraged many confessions and an opening up of information. But it has also led to some confessing minor offences in order to be released from prison, whilst continuing to deny major offences – greatly adding to the distress and fear of bereaved survivors still searching for the truth about their loved ones and now having to live alongside and face daily those they suspect of their murders.

13 Literally 'the-things-one-gets-married-with', or what we might call the 'bottom drawer'.

14 The 'Zone Turquoise' was a large area of the south-west of Rwanda to which the previous Rwandan government, army and militia had fled in June 1994, and to which the French then sent troops, ostensibly on a humanitarian mission, but in effect protecting the killers from the approaching victorious RPA. With the RPA kept out of the area by the French, very few Tutsis survived there, since the killing could continue unhindered.

15 I had been told that the captain had fled to Congo and that the colonel was awaiting trial in Arusha, Tanzania, at the International Criminal Tribunal for Rwanda set up following the genocide.

16 The Forgiveness Project, 34 Summerfield Avenue, London NW6 6JY, UK. www.theforgivenessproject.com
17 The Forgiveness Project, http://www.theforgiveness project.com/stories/jo-berry-pat-magee

The Charles Bilinda Memorial Trust

Providing Educational Opportunities and Support for Rwandans

❏ Please send me further information about the CBMT

❏ I enclose my donation of £ ....

❏ I am a tax payer and would like to Gift Aid my donation. Please send me a form.

❏ I wish to covenant .... monthly / annually (delete as appropriate)
Please send me further details

Name ....

Address ....

....

....

Please send to:
The Charles Bilinda Memorial Trust
3 Millerfield Place
Edinburgh EH9 1LW
UK
Tel: +44 (0)131 667 1568
cbmt@blueyonder.co.uk

Scottish Charity number SC023113

Tearfund

Tearfund is an evangelical Christian relief and development charity working with local partners to bring help and hope to people in need in seventy countries around the world. Christian relief and development addresses the needs of the whole person – physical, emotional, mental and spiritual. Our vision is to see lives and communities transformed by God's love. In a world of injustice, Jesus responds with compassion to meet people's needs: practical and spiritual. 'I have come that they may have life, and have it to the full (John 10:10).

If you want to be a part of Tearfund and stay in touch, please telephone or post your name and address or email.

Tearfund Head Office
100 Church Road
Teddington TW11 8QE
UK
Tel: +44 (0)845 355 8355
enquiry@tearfund.org
www.tearfund.org